Introduction by Frederick S. Wight
Catalogue by David W. Steadman

WORKS ON PAPER 1900–1960
FROM SOUTHERN CALIFORNIA COLLECTIONS

Montgomery Art Gallery
Pomona College
Claremont
September 18–October 27, 1977

M. H. de Young Memorial Museum
San Francisco
November 11–December 31, 1977

Galleries of the Claremont Colleges
Pomona College   Scripps College

This exhibition and catalogue were supported by grants from the National Endowment for the Arts, a federally supported agency, the Clyde and Eva Matson Fund of Pomona College, and an anonymous donor.

The catalogue was edited by Joanne Jaffe and designed by Lilli Cristin. All text was set in Garamond by R S Typographics. 2500 copies were printed on Warren's Lustro Dull paper by Gardner/Fulmer Lithograph.

Photography credits: Donald Hull, Los Angeles (Cat. Nos. 2, 3, 4, 7, 12, 15, 16, 19, 20, 21, 24, 26, 27, 29, 32, 33, 36, 37, 38, 39, 42, 44, 47, 50, 52, 53, 54, 55, 63, 67, 70, 72, 73, 76, 77, 78, 79); Roy Robinson, San Diego (Cat. Nos. 13, 14, 23, 25, 28, 31, 41, 43, 48, 49, 56, 58, 62, 65, 69); Frank J. Thomas, Los Angeles (Cat. Nos. 22, 34, 35, 61, 66).

Cover: Emil Nolde, *Lovers (Portrait of the Artist and His Wife)*, 1932, cat. no. 57

The catalogue entries are arranged alphabetically by artist. The illustrations are in approximately chronological order.

24472

Mrs. Nathan Alpers
Herbert and Joella Bayer
Mr. and Mrs. Michael Blankfort
Mr. and Mrs. Eli Broad
Mr. and Mrs. Philip S. Brown
Dr. and Mrs. Albert S. Chase
Mr. Douglas S. Cramer
Mr. and Mrs. Charles E. Ducommun
Constance McCormick Fearing
Fine Arts Gallery of San Diego
Mr. and Mrs. Philip Gersh
Mr. and Mrs. M. A. Gribin
Grunwald Center for the Graphic Arts,
    University of California, Los Angeles
Mr. Robert H. Halff
Mr. Carl W. Johnson
Mrs. Melville Kolliner
Dr. Vance E. Kondon
Los Angeles County Museum of Art
Margaret Mallory
Mr. and Mrs. George F. McMurray
Palm Springs Desert Museum
Mrs. Barbara R. Poe
Mr. Vincent Price
Gogi Grant Rifkind
The Robert Gore Rifkind Collection
Mr. and Mrs. H. M. Rushing
Santa Barbara Museum of Art
Scripps College
Jackie and Manny Silverman
Mr. David H. Steinmetz
Councilman Joel Wachs, Los Angeles
Louise Wilson Warren
The Weisman Collection of Art
Mr. and Mrs. Frederick S. Wight
Mr. Jack Willis
Maybelle Bayly Wolfe
Mr. and Mrs. Max Zurier
Private collections

Acknowledgments

It would have been impossible to organize an exhibition with works from over forty public and private collections without the aid of a large number of helpful people. Foremost are the private collectors who so graciously received us and who have been willing to share their drawings with all of us for over four months. We would also like to thank them for providing us with the documentary information on their drawings. Colleagues in museums have been uniformly generous in their help both in time and in information. We would like to particularly thank Betty Asher, Stephanie Barron, Maurice Bloch, Henry Gardiner, Katherine Mead, Nancy Moure, Gerald Nordland, Martin Peterson, Frederick W. Sleight, Maurice Tuchman, Betty Turnbull, and Joseph Young. We would further like to express our gratitude to James Corcoran, Joan Hazlitt, Margo Leavin, Karen Reed, Henry J. Seldis, Nicholas Wilder, and Jake Zeitlin. Special thanks should go to Joanne Jaffe and Kay Warren for organizing the documentary material.

This undertaking would not have been possible without the support of the National Endowment for the Arts and the continuing support, both financial and moral, of the administration of Pomona College.

Finally our deepest gratitude is to Mrs. Gladys Montgomery, whose generosity has turned into a reality the dream of a gallery with doubled exhibition space, a sophisticated humidity control system, and a much-needed printroom for the rapidly growing print, drawing, and photograph collections of the Claremont Colleges.

David W. Steadman

Foreword

Works on Paper 1900–1960 from Southern California Collections
is the second in a series of drawings exhibitions either organized by the Galleries of the Claremont Colleges or shared
by the Galleries with the Fine Arts Museums of San Francisco. The first exhibition in the series, held in the winter of
1976, was *18th Century Drawings from California Collections*
and the third, which will be organized by the Fine Arts
Museums of San Francisco, will be *French 19th Century
Drawings from California Collections.*

We chose the year 1960 as the terminal date of this exhibition because we plan to hold a large sequel exhibition. It
has been difficult enough to limit ourselves to 79 drawings
within this time span, and it should be clearly emphasized
that this exhibition is very much a personal selection from
the wealth of drawings from this period in Southern
California. Another curator would have created a very much
different exhibition. There are many glaring omissions of
important artists. This is not due to prior prejudices but
rather to the accidents of geography and the time at our
disposal. There are also several major collections not
represented in the exhibition, again for the same time
limitations.

One of the many pleasures in organizing this exhibition has
been the opportunity to see so many fine drawings. California may have been slow to develop collectors interested in
drawings, but it has become clear that California can be
proud of its collectors just as it is of its artists. It is mainly
for this reason that the series is devoted to drawings from
California collections. We have tried whenever possible to
include drawings of high quality which have never previously been published in the hopes that we can bring them
to the attention of a wider audience. Thus thirty-seven of
the drawings in the 18th century exhibition were previously
unpublished, and there are forty-two in this present catalogue.

D.W.S.

Introduction:

The Sinews of the Century

Europe

Nothing is more abstract, more artificial, than a line. Eyes and cameras perceive light, not lines. But even if we do not see lines, we use them. They let us organize space, and, above all, they let us surround and identify objects. A line tells us that something begins and ends, perhaps moves and lives, and is distinct from whatever lies beyond it. A line is a lasso thrown around an object.

With a line, we recognize not only the object it defines but the person who made the line. Some throw the lasso with more skill than others; they all have their own way of doing it. Their line is their signature. They have made a drawing.

The differences in drawings grow greater the closer we look. But drawings have in common (for one thing) a degree of tension, more or less tension between the object-out-there and the artist-in-here. This tension communicates itself to us.

We are never closer to an artist than when we look at a drawing. When an artist makes a painting or sculpture, it is a whole undertaking; we can stand back and think, what an accomplishment. But with a drawing, our contact with the artist is immediate; we can think, how gifted, how *accomplished.* An ineffable quality emerges from the irrelevance of size.

Painters still have a baroque attraction to large and larger events as though they were rushing to the support of an architect. The architect does not want them, of course; what an agony for a great architect to have to build a museum. There the painter is, ready and waiting with his wall. But with a drawing we forget large or small. It is an event for a cabinet.

It seems clear by now that the first half of this century saw the performance of at least two of the world's greatest artists, Matisse and Picasso. The older man seems to sum up the nineteenth century and bring it into the twentieth. Not that he looks too like the nineteenth century; the keystone of the arch has a shape of its own. Matisse is thought of as the great colorist—of all time?—in the twentieth century we must be forgiven for thinking so. But he would be considered equally great if we only possessed his drawings. He is more "modern," he is closer to us as a draftsman. Why? Not in turning white paper into light, but in something he does with anatomy. He does not give us the shape of a body or limb, but the shape or form of the motion for which body or limb was designed. Here is the source of his extraordinary animation.

The remarkable thing about Picasso—one of the remarkable things—is his capacity to distort, contort, transform to his heart's content without losing the source event. This is not exactly caricature; it is an awareness of inherited resemblance, a capacity to create a very long ancestry, a private evolution. He can take us back to a time when we wore our bones on the outside, like crustaceans. There we are with all our frightening, useful desires and a million years between our source and ourselves. Time enough for tension here.

Picasso is a formal rather than a colorful or atmospheric artist; he paints and draws like a sculptor. The effect is of concentration or condensation, a turning in as of a star imploding until its density is beyond comprehension. His concern is with the psyche rather than environment, more with time than space. This is an outgrowth of a long Spanish concern for man alone with his soul.

Before Picasso, Cubism, and the structuring tendencies of the century, a great unleashing of energy had begun, an invitation to emotion. Matisse, never basically a revolutionary, was not the sole instigator of this outburst which took a rather frantic form in France, Germany, and Italy. In France it was the Fauves, and here the name following Matisse was Rouault. In his work a strong bounding line is a border between good and evil, between life and death, between salvation and damnation.

Rouault's subject is the life of Christ. Man without God is unequal to his fate. A human judge is inevitably overweening; a king is a tragic figure with his burden of power. There is a monotony about Rouault, a narrowing, but, like the repetition in religious ritual, it is a source of strength.

For the pedagogue, Rouault often follows Matisse in a lecture series. In Cambridge it seemed self-evident (at one time) that Rouault was a great moral force, whereas Matisse was intent on happiness without compunction. To a California audience it seemed equally obvious that Matisse sensed the secret of life, and as for Rouault, he might have suffered less if he had talked to someone—was he married?

In Vienna at the beginning of the century there was less guilt and more roguery, what with an era being waltzed away and the Hapsburgs running out. Hence, Klimt. His women are rather trivial even when indulging their worst impulses. They take courage from clustering together and peek out of abstract patterns which function rather like patchwork quilts. But Vienna was where sexual guilt was invented, ironically, and if there had been no Freud, there would still have been Egon Schiele. He was one of the century's greatest draftsmen; his line is incisive. It is not a moral barrier as in Rouault; it is a barrier that must be crossed, fear losing to lust. This is a young man's art; Schiele died at twenty-eight.

This brings us to German Expressionism early and late, a phenomenon that seems as simple as rage but is rooted deep in German history. In Germany the clamor was for social reform. It was the Reformation all over again, and hence Käthe Kollwitz. But for Kollwitz there is no good answer; injustice is built into the human condition since we live to die. As surely as there is life (mother and child) there is death (skull and bones) to separate them.

Ludwig Kirchner and the *Brücke* arose in Dresden in about 1905, hard on the heels of the Fauves in France. Their Expressionism contained a legacy from Van Gogh by way of the Norwegian Edvard Munch—a show-stopping painter and printmaker steeped in the love-leads-to-death mystique. Add the great German printmaking tradition from the time of Schoengauer and Dürer. The *Brücke* artists—from Kirchner to Pechstein, to Heckel, to the older, clumsier but potent Nolde—needed forced values and uncomfortable forms, as though (especially for Kirchner) life were bedded on spikes. These artists were squashers on of color; there is a throb in their work.

Can such violence be disciplined? Yes, in the Army, and the world was at war. And, in the arts, through psychoanalysis, came a new grappling with the unconscious, a struggle to understand. The emotional turmoil of Expressionism was bound to lead to the disturbed mind as subject. We find this full strength in the work of George Grosz, depicter of murder-in-uniform complete with monocle and iron cross. Later, he came to America, and unfortunately for his art, his rage cooled and he lost his driving force.

Expressionism was not all anger. There was Oskar Kokoschka, an Austrian (or Czech), an Expressionist who lived into later times for he was coeval with Schiele. He is an artist of pathos; his early portraits and their attendant drawings are his greatest works. For Kokoschka the line gave way to the tone, the personality to landscape.

Expressionism was not solely German. The Russian Soutine had a way of combining splendid color and human pathos. Doubtless it was his early years of grinding poverty in Paris that led him to paint food: from fish to fowl, to a whole beef hanging in a butcher shop. His portraits are of haunted waifs.

The artist with a sense of the future had a choice of two twentieth-century themes: order and disorder. Both are in man's nature—a conflict destined to be with us from now on. On the one hand, there were the discoveries of mathematics, physics, biology, and the applied sciences. For man everything seemed possible. On the other hand, man was trapped by his own nature, by his zeal for murder and destruction; and, the more his nature was understood, the more discouraging the prospect.

On the side of order and structure are the artist and architect. Until the present, great architecture did not totally relinquish the architecture of anatomy; on the pediment of the Greek temple there were figures, and on the cathedral there were figures. Hidden in Cubism there were still figures. (All through Cézanne anatomy had surrendered to the simplifications of geometry.) Geometry made Cubism a complicated spectacle, so complicated that the source had to be kept simple and familiar. We find objects on a café table, or in a studio, and for Picasso the Spanish guitar, made in the image of woman.

Cubism provided a multiplicity of viewpoints, a variety of elevations as in mechanical drawing. It was description rather than literal representation. Color was artificial: grays and tans, the coloration of the clothed city body. Originally this undertaking was shared by Picasso and Georges Braque. Of course, there were other Cubists. The gifted and short-lived Juan Gris, a moon to Picasso's sun, offering light without heat, painted a steel-surfaced Cubism.

Robert Delauney introduced color into Cubism, color and architectural incoherence—for he let the Eiffel Tower lurch. The tumult he brought to Cubism appealed to the German artists. Then there was the inventor and idea man of the century, Marcel Duchamp, to whom we must return. Cubism also invaded sculpture in the works of the Russians, Archipenko and Lipchitz.

The concern with structure burst forth in Italy with the Futurists. They were less simple, less plastic, and less gifted, with the exception of Boccioni, who was killed in the war. Futurism began with a manifesto, an appeal to violence. The Futurists were for destruction, riots, and war; calamities that came to pass soon enough. Dynamism was their word. Their art was a mixed art; it was operatic. Futurism emerged in Milan. Only Balla, famous for his busy little dog on a leash, was a Roman. Severini was most like the Cubists for he had spent time in Paris.

On the eve of the First World War an art movement was brewing in Munich; its opening exhibition was in 1911–1912. Its name, the *Blaue Reiter,* came from an image of Wassily Kandinsky's. The movement was not exactly homogeneous for the figures associated with it were too gifted to coalesce. Kandinsky, a Russian, was an older man who had come to western Europe to be a painter. He began with landscapes, but at this time he was just on the verge of non-objective painting, an adventure which took him beyond the frontier where Cubism had paused. He also wrote a book, *On the Spiritual in Art,* which provided a non-objective dogma. He saw mystical qualities in art; colors, directions, up-down all held spiritual meaning. He was a musician (his instrument was the 'cello), and music for him was a metaphor for the non-representational. In his early non-representational paintings, then and through the war, a great tumult of loose forms was quite free from grav-ity—we are in the empyream moving at great speed. Later Kandinsky's compositions became more geometric, a world of mathematical forms and tensions, not of action.

The Swiss artist Paul Klee was also a late starter. He, too, had been trained as a musician (his father was a conductor), and Klee's instrument was the flute. Klee was perhaps the most imaginative man of the century. His images are sardonic and grotesque, and line can appear to falter in this world of pseudo-childhood. These lines often resemble woven patterns (his wife was a weaver), or they suggest the parallels on which musical notations are hung. The clef is a characteristic form that recurs as does a form which can be eye and lid, or sun and crescent, or seed and pod. When he visited Italy, it was less the museums than the aquarium in Naples that held his attention. Fish recur in his submerged world. A quietness, a timidity, hangs over him; he is a major artist in a minor key.

The *Blaue Reiter* painter Franz Marc painted animals in arbitrary colors: red or blue horses, red deer in the forest. He preferred animals to men for their innocence and, like Kandinsky, evaded the human. Marc, too, was killed in the war.

After the war, Kandinsky and Klee became part of the Bauhaus, the famous school of design established by the German architect Walter Gropius first in Weimar, then in Dessau. Gropius put the arts under the overall protection of architecture. The school was pragmatic, training artists for use to society; their home was no longer to be the solitary attic. Any art that could be reproduced was popular at the Bauhaus: printing, layout, photography, the design of furniture. The school produced Moholy-Nagy, and—youngest and last—Joseph Albers, who was to have a whole second phase to his creative life at Yale. The art of order had infiltrated the applied arts and was to change the look of the world, whether in building or printing.

It was to Gropius' credit that he brought together front rank artists whether or not they shared the philosophy of the school. Gropius chose Kandinsky, Oskar Schlemmer, Klee, and Lyonel Feininger; they were "form-masters" as opposed to "work-masters," that is to say, artists-in-residence. The all-purpose artist for which the school existed had yet to come into being. Such a man was Albers.

The Bauhaus had a ten-year life which ended with Hitler. The school had the Teutonic preference for order and structure. Feininger drew houses or boats but not people. Neither Kandinsky nor Klee ventured too deeply into the under-territory of the unconscious mind.

During and after the First World War artists in Russia and Holland sought a world of structure, ideas, mathematics, geometry, and physics—not Cubism, but sequels to Cubism. Suprematism and Constructivism were the names used in Russia. Kandinsky went home to Russia where the most important name, still too little appreciated, was Kasimir Malevich. In his Suprematism he stands close to Kandinsky in liberating art from representation. His *Square*

on a Square is a conception; a religious man, Malevich saw his paintings as spiritual diagrams.

Among the Russians the two remarkable brothers Naum Gabo and Anton Pevsner created a sculpture of curvilinear geometry that resembled the forms of equations of higher dimensions. Some were in bronze, but Gabo was known for his transparent events in plastic with outlying curvilinear forms made of plastic thread. These objects are astronomy or physics rendered visible; they are charged with the excitement of science.

In Holland an advanced group and its attendant publication were named *Der Stijl*. Piet Mondrian was the genius, Van Doesberg the editor-impresario, and the group included architects as well. They were all very like each other. Mondrian had been a landscape painter, but just before the war he was in Paris where he came under the spell of Cubism. He created uncompromising structures of his own, beginning with a hive of little verticals and horizontals, like plus and minus signs. Later he created structures of precise lines at right angles that enclosed fields of pure color, a red free of any admixture of blue or yellow, a yellow and blue equally untainted. Thus, each color was forever separate, and as for the lines, being at right angles, they could only meet once—forever.

At a mystical midpoint between external order and inner turmoil stands Constantin Brancusi, the Rumanian sculptor who lived and worked in Paris. His highly condensed art makes use at once of curvilinear geometry and a vaguely Oriental symbolism. The oval was his persistent form. The features of a face gradually fade until a head becomes an egg. An egg hatches and eventually becomes *Bird in Flight,* one of the century's finest conceptions. This work was "streamlined" even before the term existed. A few subtle themes worked out in wood, marble, or polished brass occupied him for a long lifetime. His pedestals are sculpture too, and he would mount a brass head on a polished brass disc so that it hovered introspectively over its own reflection. A mystic, Brancusi saw himself as a rival to Picasso.

A generation later another mystical sculptor appeared in Paris, the Swiss Alberto Giacometti. His art was still more restricted and introspective. He contented himself with a single symbol which emerged from Surrealism, a figure of infinitely tenuous proportions tied to earth with massive feet. His *Walking Man* is frail; he aspires; he is solitary; he is in motion; in a word, he is Man.

At this time, too, artists were becoming increasingly preoccupied with the man within. This introspective trend, this delving into the unconscious, was to become more and more deliberate and had its own chronology. This delving was progressive as younger men came along, for the pioneers were limited by the very anxieties that drove them.

Marc Chagall, who came to Paris from Russia (Vitebsk) before the First World War, was among these pioneers. His art is one of myth or fairytale; he is the Hans Christian Andersen of modern times. In his myths of the Russian rural ghetto people and animals talk to each other, reason enough for the animals to have more or less human faces. His people are able to fly through the air at the promptings of their imaginations. When Chagall reached Paris, his domestic astronauts became lovers. Such lovers in flight are lyric poetry, and his color is as lyrical as his theme. He has splendid stained glass windows to his credit. He has also been sustained by Old Testament subjects which are innocent, solemn, and noble. He made joy visible.

The next pre-World War I figure, Giorgio de Chirico, dug a little deeper and surfaced with an anxiety he was able to identify as the anguish of childhood. He imagines an environment for a child lost: an empty Italian city seemingly long ago abandoned to the plague. A darkened light, as of an eclipse, hangs overhead. A hidden monument, off stage, casts its long shadow across a public square. In the distance a last little train departs.

A little later, in the 1910s, de Chirico again probed this anxiety. But these paintings were less disturbing as their underlying anxiety faded. In these canvases two mannequins such as tended to inhabit studios are surrounded by the instruments of mechanical drawing, triangles and such (de Chirico's father was an engineer). Like store window dummies of a later date, these figures have no features. Yet, they definitely attract each other, and we can assume that they are de Chirico's parents. These early "metaphysical paintings" were powerful precursors of the art of anxiety.

In the midst of the war a throng of undisciplined artist-refugees congregated in neutral Switzerland, in Zurich. They had a gathering place that they called the Café Voltaire. They named their goings-on the Dada movement. Irrational behavior was applauded. They read aloud—simultaneously. The sequence of cause and effect gave way to a cult of chance.

Of the Dada group, the major talent was the sculptor and poet Jean Arp. He tore up and dropped paper to achieve random patterns. Then he turned to relatively two-dimensional cutouts which employed palette forms complete with thumbholes that he called navels. Later, as a sculptor (from about 1930) he created vaguely foetal, amorphous forms related to plant, animal, or human prototypes. He thought of these "concretions" as "torsos," for even when they had human body forms, they still lacked extremities and features. The word "bud" recurs in his titles. He imagined and created the beginnings of life.

After the war, the Dada movement shifted to Paris where it was rather forcibly killed off by a succeeding movement, Surrealism. The Dadaists' indulgence in the irrational gave way to a Parisian intellectual effort to understand the unconscious. Surrealism had its prophet, Sigmund Freud, and its mentor, the critic André Breton.

The shift from Dada to Surrealism was dramatized by the work of two major German artists on the scene. Schwitters was Dada in his way of life as well as in his art. He had an instinct for collage, for bringing together random objects which might be stubs of tickets picked up in the street. He worked with a gluepot, and when he employed a larger scale, he said that he nailed his paintings together. Schwitters, like Arp, guided the accidental with impeccable taste.

The second German artist, Max Ernst, was the greatest of the Surrealists. He was in Cologne during the war where he was joined by Arp before they both gravitated to Paris. Later, he came to America. He was a painter, draftsman, and sculptor. The irrational world he created began with collages, a clipping and rearranging of nineteenth-century wood engravings. The end product was a scene of mayhem and horror created with nail scissors. When he painted, horror continued to haunt him. In its mildest form it was a sinister Teutonic forest, but more often he painted plants for the sake of the insects and other creeping things that infested them: the life that lives under a plank. These paintings, realized with singular hothouse yellows and jaundiced greens, create an ominous life that lives off life. This is an art of acute sensibility, threat, and warning.

The artist most commonly associated with Surrealism, however, is the Spaniard, Salvador Dali. He was an illustrator of Freud. His small paintings, dating from the late 1920s, are undoubtedly his best. Just as he depended on Freud for subject matter, he depended on nineteenth-century painters (plus Vermeer) for his technique, for he was a meticulous realist. His method, therefore, is technical conservatism at the service of psychological symbolism. The Freudian concept which he most frequently exploited is that of the double image, or, the pictorial pun. He was capable of acting out Surrealism with a self-dramatization somewhat more tolerable in the theatrical profession.

The Surrealist second to Ernst in importance is the Belgian, René Magritte. Like Dali, he offers the precise depiction of an irrational event. In Magritte's world rocks can float and locomotives come out of fireplaces. The most typical Magritte ploy, however, is to create ambiguity by allowing a painted scene to function as a scene within a larger painting so that the nature of reality is called into question.

During these decades Picasso went his own way distorting the image in order to animate the psyche. In the thirties he produced some extraordinary three-dimensional heads with strange bulbous noses and bulging foreheads. These heads are entire bodies as well, with a forehead which could be read as a thigh. Characteristic also is the full face plus profile, with the head much less

distorted than the features, which appear to be loose within their general outline.

A second highly talented and a uniquely playful Spaniard was Joan Miro. He began with gnarled, dry landscapes and equally gnarled people who seemed to be made of tooled leather. He went on to adapt the infinity of objects in Dutch seventeenth-century interiors and to give them new life in the imp fairytales he invented. He then invented a cosmos of his own with sun and moon symbols and interpenetrating amoeba-like forms: sex under the microscope. His grotesques often suggest whiskery old women, peasant matriarchs like vultures disturbed on their nests. His decorative art grew to a mural scale, and he also moved on to sculpture. He is the last of the generation of the century's pioneers of genius.

Marcel Duchamp, early and late, was like no one else, the idea man of his time who only produced by fits and starts. Before the world knew what Cubism was, Duchamp had passed through it; his *Nude Descending a Staircase* is a preview of Surrealism. He produced images which comment on the series of tubes we all are and which, in retrospect, suggest the handiwork of the open heart surgeon. In Duchamp love and plumbing are hard to separate. He set discs in motion to produce kinetic art, and he tangled up a gallery with an endless cord to produce a species of three-dimensional Jackson Pollock. He left behind him a curious peep show, an unreachable voyeuristic image.

Duchamp understood that the important matter for the artist of the twentieth-century was the idea, and he pioneered almost all the pictorial ideas. When he wanted pure relationships he played chess.

In England only a few artists threw off the nineteenth century and escaped from the influence of an age of literature. Those few who did escaped all the way into plastic events. Sculpture turned out to be the great British contribution to the art of the twentieth century despite the fact that England had had no significant sculpture since the Middle Ages. And, sculptors, of course, drew.

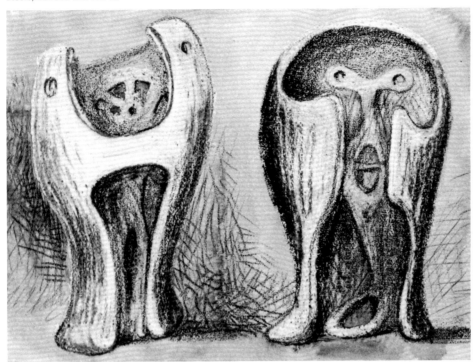

Epstein, originally an American, was a modern precursor who came early in
the century. Even before the First World War he sensed the formal changes
that were brewing. They liberated him, but he did not contribute to them.
Rather, his images were vaguely archaic and privately primitive, like the
images of Gauguin, and finally he settled for an intense, animated
portraiture.

The century's great British sculptor is Henry Moore. It is hard to think of
him as a Surrealist; his work seems so primeval. There is more than a trace
of "primitive" art in it, especially a Pre-Columbian influence. His great
personal contribution is a sense of time past, not the eon-long evolutionary
time of Picasso, but an historic time long enough for the eroding of stone.
His figures look like thousand-year-old effigies, their features all but oblit-
erated, as though the pounding sea has been at work upon them.

A persistent theme for Moore is the reclining woman. This develops into the
theme of mother and child, and a male parent is added to round out the
family trilogy.

During the war, Moore created an extraordinary series of drawings of
Londoners sleeping in the underground stations, white lines on a dark
field. They lie in a tube-womb, stubbornly clinging to life. No one who
has stepped over these prone people forgets them, and Moore arrested
the experience.

Moore's father was a Yorkshire miner, and there is something of the miner in
Moore's intensity when he attacks wood or stone. The human body is com-

posed of hollows, the largest inside the rib cage. The thorax actually rings hollow, and Moore (as though he were tapping and listening) time and again leaves the chest cavity open. Also, in his female figures he creates a midway partition, or dike, which serves to separate the form into distinct sculptural events. Ultimately, these two forms were to draw apart. His sense of man's inner life comes to a crisis when he deals with the skull as a housing for the machinery of the senses, which he often envisages as separate organs able to peer out.

Somewhere between Moore and Arp is Barbara Hepworth who creates with an elegant abstraction a family of living forms all her own.

When it comes to two dimensions, Augustus John had a vital if loose draftsmanship. Wyndham Lewis created a movement of his own, Vorticism, a species of Cubism which had an inherent vitality. Ben Nicholson evolved a highly personal Cubism working with geometric forms often in very low relief that share the tasteful brown and tan tonalities of Braque. Graham Sutherland created a spikey, grotesque Cubism, mostly of plant forms that are thorny, uncomfortable, and often effectively rendered in black and yellow. But the British painter of the century is Francis Bacon.

Bacon's art is a powerful and ominous account of sadistic human intentions, conscious and unconscious. Murder and "crucifixion" parade in terms inescapably sexual and compulsive. His figures are usually trapped in a sort of torture chamber or transparent box, like Eichman at his trial. Anything else, the artist implies, is illusion and escape, the suburbs of the psyche in which we imagine we live.

Italy has produced important sculptors. The most winsome, Giacomo Manzù, is very kind to women. The most important, Marino Marini, has also been a prolific draftsman. He is a stubborn adherent to a single theme, the man on horseback. His horse and rider can be seen as a mockery of Fascism, for the man is a bewildered little creature, unwarlike, not dangerous, who exists in a state of childish, astonished ecstasy. The connotations are highly sexual; it is an art of erectile tissue which offers less variety than an art of muscle and bone.

Italy produced two painters of great distinction, one early and one late in the century, who seem to exist not to sustain the times but to embellish them. The first, Amadeo Modigliani, was born in Pisa and worked and died in Paris. To be tubercular, dissipated, and die young was something of a nineteenth-century romantic ideal, and such was Modigliani's existence. He began as a sculptor, working with and influenced by Brancusi. He adopted Brancusi's addiction to the oval form and produced a single image, the caryatid. His illness diverted him from carving to painting, and he created portraits, more often of women than men, and occasional nude figures. Influenced by Italian Mannerism, his images are strangely elongated and have an exoticism of their own. His distortions tend toward monotony, but he never loses the personality of the sitter, and he has done much to populate a solipsistic, though great period. Modigliani drew superbly. His images are frail, aloof, intensely alive, and sufficiently typical to invite forgery.

The second major Italian artist, Morandi, was the century's recluse. He compulsively produced still lifes based on a single theme: bottles on a table. The Chardin of his generation, his paintings and drawings have a quality of their own which suggests that privacy and perfection go well together.

America

About the time of the Fauves and the first beginnings of the Cubist Movement in Paris, a breakthrough took place in American art. It seemed equally portentous although it was hardly more than a change in subject matter. It was a burly rejection of the refinements of nineteenth-century taste.

This new vigor was largely due to the newspaper illustrators, the painters and draftsmen who had covered the Spanish War in Cuba. They created, or at least perpetuated, a new American image that had been dramatized by Theodore Roosevelt as a "rough rider" and had allowed Americans to see themselves as heroes in a western. The war over, these illustrators turned their attention back to the life of the city streets, the waterfront, the bars, and the prize fighting ring.

A group of these illustrator-war correspondents had been working on the Philadelphia Press under art editor Edward Davis, and when Davis moved to the New York area, they trailed along. In Philadelphia they had been influenced by a young painter, Robert Henri, who had seen Paris and had taken a good look at Manet. Although Henri was not a great painter, he offered self-confidence to the group of illustrators discovering they were artists. He, too, went to New York where he was to become an important teacher.

These younger Philadelphians submitted their work to the annual exhibition of the National Academy of Design and were promptly rejected, whereupon Henri withdrew his own entries. A New York dealer then asked Henri to put together an exhibition of the rejected, and Henri assembled The Eight, who were at once labeled the Ash Can School. Like most objects in an ash can they were not too alike, nor were they to be long together. They included Everett Shinn, William Glackens, George Luks, Maurice Prendergast, and a young man from Ohio, George Bellows.

Prendergast developed a late Impressionism of his own. He created tapestry effects out of throngs of people in parks or at beaches; his faceless generalizations were written in over tan and green tonal harmonies of great distinction.

A complete antithesis to Prendergast was Bellows, a dynamic younger painter who attacked the city scene with animated brushwork. His action-packed canvases were vital and arresting; his drawings and lithographs were either sunlit or floodlit; shadows were black; the effect was bold, and his success was immediate.

Just before the First World War, early in 1913, the American art world treated itself to the famous Armory Show in which whatever was new in Europe, through Cubism, burst on an unprepared public. The effect on artists was overwhelming and on critics infuriating. Among the critics, strangely enough, was Theodore Roosevelt, who came up with the phrase "the lunatic fringe."

Perhaps with some feeling of a revolutionary left behind, Bellows was to formalize his painting. He introduced an artificial structuring device, dynamic symmetry, which he borrowed from a theory of Jay Hambidge. Following this theory he cut the canvas into triangles that pinpointed spots deserving of special attention in the composition. But for Bellows the result was far from dynamic. As his paintings lost their vital brushwork and became set pieces, their animation was eclipsed. What the final results of these experiments might have been cannot be known for he died in his early forties. He left an impressive body of work.

Although Edward Hopper was the same age as Bellows, by the time Bellows' life was over Hopper had just begun to realize his more somber abilities. There was a certain confusion in the 1920s between an American way of seeing and an American subject, but both were especially characteristic of Hopper. He painted American buildings in the city and in rural New England and fixed on them an almost fetishistic attention as though he were in pursuit of the-house-where-I-was-born. An American loneliness was his theme, often expressed by means of intense light, either a midday glare or the corner light of a city at night. The result is a *Look Homeward, Angel* cry of longing and disappointment.

The era of modern art in America did not date from the Armory Show but from the activities of Alfred Steiglitz, a photographer, dealer, and impresario who opened a gallery, "291 Fifth Avenue," before the First World War. He moved his gallery twice, and it eventually became known as "An American Place." He first showed photographs, turned to Rodin watercolors, and then presented the first Picasso to be shown in this country. But soon he was only showing Americans: Max Weber, Marsden Hartley, Arthur Dove, John Marin, Georgia O'Keeffe—all major figures. Ultimately, he only showed the latter three.

John Marin had a gradual growth. He had planned to be an architect before he went to Europe to become an artist. Like many other Americans before the First World War, he had little awareness of what was coming in Paris; he made modest Whistler-influenced etchings, and it was not until he came home that he discovered the American scene and light and began in earnest his long watercolor career. He first painted New York skyscrapers and then a New England landscape and rugged seascape as he moved further and further along the coast of Maine. He pursued essentials, and his scenes are highly simplified. As he disliked a square format, he would slash in hexagonal borders, and time and again bold lines cut across the view like window bars. He had diagrams for certain effects, such as distant trees or rain in the sky. Often several scenes or objects appear on one paper as in photo-montage. And, he would use a black sun for contrast.

Late in his long life he turned to oil paint, keeping much of his bold watercolor technique, and ultimately, he produced "writings" made of tangled lines of paint ejected through a syringe. The result was a capturing of a brittle American excitement, a sophisticated view of a frontier.

Arthur Dove was the most advanced American painter of his generation. He gave up illustration to pursue his own highly personal images. His "Nature Symbolized" series of 1911 is coeval with Kandinsky's turn from relatively legible abstraction to the non-objective. Dove, however, had no need of the geometric; his forms were organic, and he stayed with the symbol.

Dove had an endless struggle with poverty, whether on the Connecticut shore, or in his home territory of upper New York state, or living aboard a yawl on Long Island Sound (the boat was paid for by the actor William S. Hart). Although his paintings are small, especially those painted below deck in his boat, they make cosmic statements with their symbols for suns, moons, storms, and even the sounds of foghorns rolling over the water. In the twenties he made little three-dimensional portraits constructed of items associated with his subjects. An organic coiling and flowing characterizes his imagery which translates the world of growth and weather much as Arp's imagery translates growth and anatomy. No American artist was larger in spirit.

Georgia O'Keeffe, Charles Sheeler, Charles Demuth, Niles Spencer were to be seen either at Steiglitz' or at the Downtown Gallery, where the dealer Edith Halpert showed only American art. These painters shared a sharp, linear, cleansed vision and in consequence were called the Precisionists. O'Keeffe shared something of Dove's involvement with symbols. For a while she painted greatly enlarged flowers that seemed to possess all the sexual attraction that flowers presumably offer to hummingbirds. Her art became more stark, more intensely personal when she moved to New Mexico. There, she was able to capture with an incandescent clarity the vast spaces of the Southwest. She could convey the desert and its way of life with a bleached bone. Her painting possesses immense dignity and assurance.

Charles Sheeler came from Pennsylvania, and he worked with all the austerity of a Pennsylvania Dutch furniture maker. He was an excellent photographer which tended to carry over in a sharp focus approach to paper or canvas. He was far from abstract, but he did allow himself double images—the equivalent of the multiple exposure in photography. His subjects were the farm and American industry. His paintings of industry are uncontaminated by dirt, sweat, or even employees; it is the investor's vision. The only human figure in all of Sheeler's work is himself, seated, seen from the back. Yet, this cold, meticulous art was produced by a highly emotional man. With his respect for artifact and machinery, he came closer than any humanist to depicting the American dream.

Charles Demuth was two artists in one. He painted slight watercolor illustrations that dealt with acrobats and the burlesque, and with the writings of Zola and Henry James. His watercolors for James' *Turn of the Screw* are worthy of the writing; they have all the elegance of Paul Klee. Then Demuth painted still lifes—fruit, vegetables, and flowers—watercolors of a crystaline elegance.

None of this prepares us for his turn to the American industrial scene; here he is at his best in a view of grain elevators, *My Egypt*. Demuth (like Feininger) created a nest of rays or a penumbra of straight lines to provide an ambiance for his architecture. In much the same manner he painted a famous little symbol, *I Saw the Figure Five in Gold*. This figure was the number on a fire engine rushing by, and the painting illustrated (or perhaps we should say illuminated) a poem by his friend William Carlos Williams.

The great Depression between the World Wars had a devastating effect on the arts. The Roosevelt government stepped in to provide employment for the artist in a studio program or in producing the American Index of Design. The Administration tried to decentralize art since New York had ceased to be a market, and in consequence a great many nondescript murals went into post offices. Obviously, the government found it easier to encourage representation than to endorse abstraction, and as American art became even more self-consciously national, the trend was sharply away from Europe. It is touching in retrospect to see paintings depicting America at work when there was no work. What hope the artist had was a liberal hope in a liberal government, and he now felt an influence from south of the border, from the Mexican muralists Rivera and Orozco, who were talking directly to the Indian by way of the wall.

A similar down-to-earth art emerged at this time in the Midwest. Thomas Benton, John Steuart Curry, and Grant Wood were the major names. Benton had studied in Paris, but when he came home he threw off the influence of Europe to become "All American." He produced murals for his native state of

Missouri, for the Whitney Museum of American Art, and for the New School for Social Research in New York. He created a Bret Hart western of Missouri and the Ozarks, a scene of men in overalls and women in bonnets. He provided his cast with a lank, rangy anatomy that verged on the comic strip. With their folkways they have great animation and vitality.

John Steuart Curry created farm scenes in the Ash Can tradition. His best, or best-known work, *Baptism in Kansas,* is a document in frontier literature. Later he pushed drama toward melodrama, notably in his whirlwind portrait of John Brown.

Grant Wood also went to Europe where he discovered the northern Flemish artists. From Van Eyck to Memling they provided him with a ready-made style, crisp and unrelenting, with which he felt he could do justice to the life of the farm that he had known in the Midwest. One of the results was a famous canvas, *American Gothic,* that he painted in 1930. Such a subject matter and style, however, was an invitation to the picturesque. Given a successful idea like his *Parson Weems,* he was arresting, but his landscapes were often needle-point quaint.

The Mexican mural influence weighed heavily upon Rico Lebrun. He grew up in Naples, and his paintings—progressively larger until they reached mural scale—are somber, often with black grounds inherited from sixteenth-century Neopolitan art. His images, half symbol, half grotesque anatomy, owe much to Goya and Picasso. All these influences fuse in his large mural of the *Crucifixion,* an imposing, if eclectic, treatment of a great theme.

Ben Shahn was stirred by social injustice and the evils of the Depression. He was born in Russia and brought up in New York in the midst of hard times. He was an illustrator, postermaker, muralist, and photographer, and at all times a protestor for human rights. His forceful drawing verges on caricature, his color serving only to heighten communication. His limitations are the limitations of the propagandist. In America it is more patriotic to look up and is often considered subversive to look down.

It was inevitable that the arts of the western world, of Europe and America, would fuse once more in spite of wars and hard times. The Museum of Modern Art and the Whitney Museum of American Art had opened just in time for the Depression, and although they could not carry the American artist through the crisis, they could and did encourage his sense of mission. An international aesthetic reemerged, a sense that the art of the twentieth century should be highly personal and inventive and should relate more to an epoch than to a place.

No American better represented this new concern than Stuart Davis. The son of Edward Davis, the art editor of the Philadelphia Press, Stuart was just old enough to exhibit in the Armory show and to be mightily influenced by it. He used flat, vivid colors to describe New York or Rockport, Massachusetts, and in his determination to come to grips with essentials, he nailed a glove and an eggbeater to a table, added an electric fan, and sat down before his subject for a year.

He went to Paris and painted the city with his poster-like technique that had nothing to do with French art. A transition to the completely abstract followed. In place of objects he introduced letters and words, either real or invented. He was influenced by American jazz, and his flat color was strident and piercing. His paintings recall the main streets of an American small town with its blatant billboards or the neon blaze of an American city seen from a descending plane at night. Just as all French artists, regardless of their methods, look up to Delacroix and Poussin, American artists, early and late, have admired Davis.

Arshile Gorky was fortunate in his friendships with Stuart Davis and de Kooning. At sixteen he had come to America from his native Armenia, and his relatively short life was spent in the midst of the Depression. His painting reveals continuous experimentation. He turned away from the formalized representation that characterized Cubism in America and produced colorful fantasies closer to the early work of Kandinsky and Miro. His brilliant flattened shapes are animated and sensual. They tend to be outlined—almost written in—and seem to be tied down by fine black lines like so many flying kites. He was on the Surrealist route leading to Abstract Expressionism when an accident was followed by suicide when he was forty-three.

An art form essentially American emerged in the 1940s and continued into the 1950s. Until this time the most advanced American artists would have had to admit to formative influences from Europe. Now at last a native art was to emerge, a direct reflection of the artist's personality independent of the American scene. This now familiar movement was given the name Abstract Expressionism.

The artist most frequently associated with this movement was Jackson Pollock. Everyone knows how his paintings were made: how he dripped paint from the end of a stick onto a canvas laid on the floor. The total effect was of swirling lines as luminous as the milky way, as continuous as life, and without apparent finite limits. Pollock's painting was an activity, a process; the critic Harold Rosenberg gave it a subtitle: Action Painting.

Pollock's bold early paintings of the 1940s had borne some resemblance to the more abstract swirls of the Mexican mural painter Orozco. By 1947 these swirls had refined themselves into Pollock's now familiar hazy cosmologies. Despite (or because of) his success, his last years were relatively unproductive. In his few late canvases great black gargoyle heads peer out, as unexpected as they are ominous. Like the late black paintings of Goya, they appear too compulsive to have been welcome. Death ended this phase by way of an automobile accident, but a revolution had taken place.

The Abstract Expressionist movement was surprisingly short lived. Perhaps it seemed too easy, too much as though anything would do. But like all other art forms, it was only done well by a few, and they tended to be the forerunners. Next to Pollock, the two most impressive of the group were Willem de Kooning and Robert Motherwell. De Kooning, who came to America from Rotterdam, began with figurative paintings, tenuous and tonal. However abstract he may appear, he remained vaguely figurative in the sense that there was something *there*. He is most famous for his *Woman* series which are decidedly action paintings. In them a fierce, grotesque giantess appears in the midst of a lather of violent paint. She is deliberately fragmented and seems half submerged by the surrounding slashings.

There are also more abstract canvases with impressive, congested black coiling forms, vaguely organic. And, there are still more abstract landscapes composed not of objects but of glaring lights: blues, yellows, salmon pinks. De Kooning presents Abstract Expressionism as impulse, but it is a willful, guided impulse.

Robert Motherwell came to painting late, as a means of expressing ideas. He had been trained in philosophy at Harvard and took a special interest in aesthetics. He was in contact with European Surrealists who had come to this country as refugees, Ernst and Matta among others.

Abstract Expressionism appealed to painters who had gone the Cubist route and were seeking a more personal gesture. But it also claimed the later Surrealist painters who emerged after the unconscious had already been illustrated and who thought in terms of forms or symbols that were charged with the power of the obscure. Motherwell found such symbols in black ovals caught between black columns in his series *Elegy for the Spanish Republic.* Like a classical colonnade, these forms allowed the painter to evoke a horizontal infinity. They are altogether grand, and they provided Motherwell with a central theme for a decade.

If these large, dark silhouettes are the base of Motherwell's composition, the treble is an infinite number of smaller collages in which one sees the artist's concern with Dada—with chance. Like Arp, like Schwitters, who believed they were relying on chance, Motherwell has been able to guide the accidental for he has unerring taste.

Motherwell's philosophic training and intelligent approach allowed him to become a spokesman for the abstract artists of his generation. He had sufficient detachment and ability to survive the coming and going of Abstract Expressionism. His taste rescues him from the obstreperousness of impulse; he is not the prisoner of a style.

Franz Kline made bold black on white attacks on large canvases. It is said that he once projected a small work and realized the latent power in the increase in scale. His images look like greatly magnified Japanese script, which may bear on the fact that his paintings are admired in Japan. He came from the coal mining region of Pennsylvania (he began with representational scenes of the downtrodden), and in his severe black and white compositions some have felt that they detected seams of coal in the rock. Most artists eventually outgrow their self-imposed limitations, and late in life Kline abandoned black and white for color.

Clyfford Still, like Motherwell, came from the Northwest, from the state of Washington and from Alberta. In his large, effective canvases—turgid and shaggy with brushwork—one color comes through another as though through a tear in the surface. These personal statements, like the artist himself, are essentially hostile to art history; like the scenes of their origin, they are primeval, and that is their strength.

Philip Guston (born in Los Angeles) has been sporadically, if impressively, an Abstract Expressionist. His early paintings were of an animated American scene organized into Cubist patterns. When he became abstract, he produced highly personal images that tended to occupy a central circular area of the canvas. Here, brushstrokes coil together, typically red on a gray field; the effect suggests the image of the retina as seen by an oculist. These are beautiful paintings, sensitive and free of the stridency of the Abstract Expressionist movement.

Adolph Gottlieb was long occupied with personal hieroglyphics, private symbols stored in a series of compartments. Then he simplified and enlarged his canvas. Typically, he places a circular image above its reflection, the upper a fiery sun, the lower a dark furry area. This can be read as a sun above a troubled earth, or as twin stars—bright versus dark—or as transparency versus opacity, or as a luminous event above a disturbed base.

In contrast to these painters, different as personalities yet related in theory, is a somewhat alien figure, the German painter Hans Hofmann. For most of his long life he was a teacher with his own art school in and out of Munich before and after the First World War. By 1930 he had come to America. Friends at Berkeley brought him to California where he taught and exhibited, and he reestablished his school in New York and in Provincetown during the summers. Scores of students experienced his schooling and listened to his theory of painting. Central to his teaching was the notion of "push and pull" by which he meant that warm colors advance and cool retreat, a perception that takes us back to Cézanne. For Hofmann, however, this idea was all-important. He saw the forward and backward thrust within the canvas as far outweighing any sense of lateral movement. Composition was, therefore, a matter of tension among colors.

In comparison with other Abstract Expressionist paintings, Hofmann's do not suggest infinity; they are merely large. He was seen as something of an outsider by other abstractionists, all the more so as he had hardly begun to paint before coming to America. But, when he began, he was enormously productive and made up for lost time. He painted and drew with gusto, and his strength was in his color sense. In Abstract Expressionist days when no one realized that color as an end in itself was soon to have its day, Hofmann's characteristic orange-reds, apple-greens, and intense blues were a resplendent experience. He ranged from slashing and tumultuous brushwork to adjacent fields of ringing color.

The youngest, or latest, of the Abstract Expressionists was the Californian Sam Francis. His early images are cellular: brilliant corpuscular or amoeboid forms with spottings or splashings of arresting color; vivid blues or purples are set off against yellows or reds on a white ground. The whole creates a throbbing sensation in which the onlooker feels submerged. That Francis was a latecomer to the abstract mode was no obstacle, and as time has proven, he was keeping pace with the coming concerns: the limited means of minimal art and color as employed in color field painting. His paintings are large in scale among large scale painting, and he is international in spirit. He won his first recognition in Europe and is equally well-known and understood in Japan.

If Pollock led the way into Abstract Expressionism, Mark Rothko leads out. His paintings are juxtaposed tones of color; the canvases are vertical with a horizontal bar or space between two color tones. The effect is of a window with a horizontal sash bar, or with a shade lowered halfway. This single format is a stage for some of the most beautiful color harmonies imaginable. With the passage of time these tones grew more muted, more somber. Lines vanished, so did strokes. Such paintings have a mystical splendor that derives from their resolution into two ultimates, two tones which can only symbolize the final duality—life and death. Gradually, as these tones darken, death wins.

In Europe an "advanced" way of seeing is a minority activity although in retrospect the new vision will appear to have been what the times were about. In America, movements and trends have been somewhat more unionized. Often artists seem willing to interrupt their own growth, giving in to the pressure to conform. The problem is compounded by the fact that movements are shorter than a lifetime and come and go. The mere fact—the very existence—of Abstract Expressionism presupposed that there were other, persisting, forms of expression.

Milton Avery was a painter with a highly personal vision. He changed very little, and then in relation to his own earlier work. He would translate a literal scene into highly generalized outlines, so generalized that the elements of landscape or seascape became mere symbols; his figures became a single consolidated gesture and assumed an unexpected sense of mass. He remained faithful to this way of painting while his friends were developing the new abstraction. He was thought to have been influenced by Matisse, but if so, his painting was much cooler and more poetic.

Mark Tobey was a Midwesterner who worked in the Seattle region at an important time in his development. He had been a portrait painter in New York but later came under the spell of Oriental art. He had traveled widely in Europe and in the Far East, and the Orient worked a radical change upon him. He became converted to the Baha'i religion, took up Chinese brush painting in the 1920s, and began to explore Zen Buddhism in the 1930s. Out of this new interest came a new technique, his "white writing," a luminous maze on a dark ground. Tobey's "writing" suggests a glyphic language which seems to precede written communication. Other artists, not only Pollock but Marin as well, were exploring this new twentieth century resource. But Tobey use it to create his own spiritual ambience.

Richard Diebenkorn is a West Coast painter, from Oregon, to San Francisco, to Los Angeles. His interests are essentially abstract, but it is an abstraction not far removed from an underlying physical reality. He painted in San Francisco when both Rothko and Still were teaching there and an abstract movement was under way. Diebenkorn's early abstraction utilized very free brushwork, strong linear patterns, and islands of color. Often landscapes lurked under these rich patterns, and the time came when Diebenkorn (and confederates calling themselves the San Francisco School) turned to figures in an environment. For Diebenkorn this environment was often the geometry of a containing room. But such an uneasy balance between the figure and the geometry of architecture was not to last, and ultimately the geometry (re-sembling large land divisions seen from the air) was to become his dominant expression.

Meanwhile, in his black and white drawings, Diebenkorn followed two distinct routes: his bold, generalized figure pieces and his geometric structures. Both expressions are of equal power.

David Smith, a Midwesterner, is by general consent thought of as the outstanding twentieth-century American sculptor. He was a riveter and welder in a Studebaker plant at nineteen and during the Second World War worked for the American Locomotive Company—a background that suited his rugged biography. He chose Bolton Landing on Lake George as his home territory and strewed the fields with major sculptures that seem to rise out of the ground like natural outcroppings—a relation of sculpture to environment also favored by Henry Moore.

Smith had an early interlude as a painter which may account for his liking for paint on sculpture. He favored a strong red, like the red lead seen on structural steel. This experience as a painter must have something to do, too, with the arresting quality of his drawings that are another product of his conceptions.

All this suggests an instinct for three dimensions and a husky scale. But, for a long while Smith's sculptures were small, rather open, and meant to be seen from a single point of view, again reflecting the painter's instinct. Only in his last years did he turn to the monumental, and ultimately to a "Cubi" series composed of four square stainless steel beams. They are welded together where they touch and seem to cling to each other by some inner magnetism. Their stainless steel surfaces are scored in shimmering patterns, an embellishment as illogical as it is effective. What might have followed this tremendously successful venture into the grandiose is unknown for Smith died in an automobile accident in 1965 at the height of his achievement.

Other names come to mind, and for every name two more deserve to be included. But this essay can be no more than an overview of a period. It is a reminder that artists are individuals—and how drawings insist upon it—but individuals who share a time so that there is justification in showing them as an expression of a particular century, their own.

It is difficult to escape the feeling that an exhibition so rich in drawings narrows the gap between artist and onlooker. Many of the works seem somehow an ongoing activity between the two, broken off as in conversation once the point has been made. Such a drawing exists as an intention that suddenly needs no further elaboration; it reaches successfully beyond itself—as an idea or as a gesture of a personality.

Frederick S. Wight

The catalogue entries are arranged alphabetically by artist. The illustrations are in approximately chronological order.

MILTON AVERY
American, 1893–1965

1

Seaside Haircut, 1948 (ill. p. 120)
Watercolor
Signed and dated, bottom right corner: "Milton Avery 1948"
29½ x 22 in. (74 x 55.8 cm.)
Provenance: Mrs. Richard Nelson, Palm Springs
Lent by the Palm Springs Desert Museum, Gift of
Mrs. Richard Nelson

Milton Avery has been characterized as "a lyric poet in
the New England tradition."[1] Like many New England
poets—one thinks particularly of Robert Frost—his art was
deceptively simple, concerned primarily with the everyday
events of his world: landscapes, people at leisure, interiors.

One of his many recurrent themes was that of the simple act
of the haircut. In this watercolor version of 1948, we see
him combining and flattening shapes, those of the people
and the background—a decorative two-dimensional surface
built up of abstracted rocks and sea.

There is, however, more sense of movement here than is
usual in Avery's work. We feel the strain and weight on the
woman's left leg even though her body is treated as a flat
shape. As in other beach scenes by Avery the man is much
darker in color than the woman.

[1]Frederick S. Wight, *Milton Avery,* Baltimore Museum of
Art, 1953, p. 4.

HERBERT BAYER
German/American, b. 1900

2

Violin and Frames, 1928 (ill. p. 96)
Pen and ink
Signed and dated, bottom right: "Herbert Bayer 16.7"
Titled and dated, on verso: "Violin and Frames 7/1928"
10 x 13⅜ in. (25.4 x 34 cm.)
Literature: *Herbert Bayer, Book of Drawings,* Chicago, 1961,
No. 2
Lent by Herbert and Joella Bayer

Herbert Bayer was a student at the Bauhaus, and from 1925
to 1928 he taught typography and design there. With
Walter Gropius and Moholy-Nagy he designed the exhibition of *Deutscher Werkbund* at the Grand Palais in Paris in
1930. Later in that decade all three men came to America.

Bayer is a painter, photographer, typographer, designer, and
architect. In each of these fields he has adhered to the
Bauhaus philosophy that art should be integrated with life.
The imagery in his art has been called "working signs."
"His visions have tentacles reaching into the world of the
spectator...these signs are our signs and we are made to
visualize new possibilities of making them WORK."[1]

In *Violin and Frames* Bayer overlaps thin planes, like sheets
of glass, so that we see the violin (singular, not plural) in
differently shaded slices. We, thus, have a multiple vision of
an object and a planar structure emphasized in the frames;
both are inherited from Synthetic Cubism.

[1]Alexander Dorner, *Way Beyond "Art"—the Work of Herbert
Bayer,* New York, 1947, p. 139.

GEORGE BELLOWS
American, 1882–1925

3

Street Scene, c. 1910 (ill. p. 68)
Pencil, ink, and crayon
Signed in pencil, bottom left: "Geo Bellows"
Inscribed in brown ink, bottom left on margin: "To Major
Simson/Geo Bellows"
6 x 9 in. (15.2 x 22.8 cm.)
Exhibitions: Fine Arts Gallery of San Diego, "The Young
Collection," January, 1974; exhibited annually since 1946 at
Scripps College
Literature: Lang Art Gallery, Scripps College, *American
Painting 1870–1930: The Collection of General and Mrs.
Edward Clinton Young,* Claremont, California, 1946, No. 1;
Lang Art Gallery, Scripps College, *The Young Collection,*
Claremont, California, 1971, No. 1
Lent by Scripps College, Gift of General and Mrs. Edward
Clinton Young, 1946

George Bellows became a nationally acclaimed artist at the
age of twenty-seven in 1909 when he was elected Associate
Member of the National Academy of Design, the youngest
man ever so honored. In 1913 he became a full member
of the National Academy and in the same year was one of
the organizers of the famous Armory exhibition which
introduced modern European art for the first time to an
American audience.

It was between these years that Bellows produced the
drawing *Street Scene.* It is typical of his best drawings in the
artist's use of a large variety of materials within a single
work to achieve pictorial completeness. Although there are
touches of colored crayon, color is completely subordinated
to a linear conception.

1 George Bellows, *Under the Elevated,* watercolor, Museum of Modern Art, New York, Gift of Abby Aldrich Rockefeller

The drawing is directly related to one of the few watercolors Bellows ever made, *Under the Elevated* (fig. 1). Both show the same horse and leader clearing the snow, bypassers at the right, a boat docked in the background, and the elevated overhead. In the drawing, however, falling snow is indicated by thin, white crayon lines.

Bellows kept careful records of the dates of his paintings and lithographs (which he began making only in 1916). There is, however, little precise knowledge of the chronology of his drawings. The related watercolor has tentatively been dated before 1910.[1] The drawing is close in subject matter to three paintings of the early teens: *Snow Dumpers* in the Columbus Gallery of Fine Arts, *Docks in Winter* in the collection of Miss Helen Frick, both of 1911, and *Men of the Docks* of 1912 at Randolph-Macon Women's College.

[1]Carl O. Schniewind, *George Bellows,* The Art Institute of Chicago, 1946, No. 94.

THOMAS HART BENTON
American, 1889–1976

4

Saturday Afternoon, c. 1939 (ill. p. 113)
Pencil, pen, and black ink and brown wash
Signed, bottom right corner: "Benton"
8½ x 11½ in. (21.6 x 29.2 cm.)
Provenance: James Graham Gallery, New York
Lent by Mr. and Mrs. George F. McMurray

Thomas Hart Benton achieved his greatest success as a mural painter in the 1930s with those at the Missouri State Capital of 1936 being his best known.

In 1939 at approximately the time of this drawing, Benton was living in Missouri but was traveling around the United States. *Saturday Afternoon* is a quintessential American scene of the 1930s: the small town street is flanked by one-story wood buildings; Model T Fords are parked while people amble along the sidewalks. It is close in style and subject to the drawing *Ozark Town* of 1939.[1]

[1]No. 118 in Matthew Baigell's *Thomas Hart Benton,* New York, 1973.

MARC CHAGALL
Russian, b. 1887

5

Card Players, 1917 (ill. p. 83)
Pencil, watercolor, and tempera
Signed and dated, bottom right: "Chagall 1917"
9½ x 15⅜ in. (24.1 x 40 cm.)
Provenance: Mr. and Mrs. William Preston Harrison
Exhibitions: Art Institute of Chicago, 1932, 1941;
F. Meyer, 294
Literature: Los Angeles County Museum of Art, *Drawings in the Collection of the Los Angeles County Museum of Art,* 1970 (ill., n.p.)
Lent by the Los Angeles County Museum of Art, The Mr. and Mrs. William Preston Harrison Collection

Chagall arrived in Paris from his native Russia in 1910. His paintings of 1911–1912 were his first great works in which dream and fantasy images were combined with natural objects. As André Breton has written, "In 1911 and through Chagall alone, metaphor made its triumphal entry into modern painting."[1]

In 1914 he returned to Russia to live in Petrograd, and after the October Revolution of 1917, returned to his native town of Vitebsk. During the winter of that year Chagall painted three of his most famous figurative compositions: *Double Portrait with Wine Glass, Over the Town,* and *The Promenade.*

The figure of the seated man with the strongly arched back goes back to Chagall's painting *The Holy Coachman* of 1911–1912 (fig. 2). That painting was hung upside down in Chagall's one-man show in Berlin in 1914. The artist allowed it to remain that way permanently. Seen in its original position, as it is illustrated here, the young man with the scroll arches his back as if inspired; the crown on his head reaches down to the buildings below. This same figure was also used in a small oil painting which, like this watercolor, dates from 1917.[2]

[1]Quoted in Werner Haftmann, *Marc Chagall,* New York, 1973, p. 7.
[2]It is mentioned, but not illustrated, in Haftmann, p. 26.

2 Marc Chagall, *The Holy Coachman*, 1911–1912, private collection, The painting is reproduced upside down, but in the way Chagall painted it

GIORGIO de CHIRICO
Italian, 1888–1976

6

Metaphysical Interior with Fish Molds, 1916 *(ill. p. 81)*
Pencil
Signed, bottom left: "de Chirico"
13 x 10¼ in. (33 x 26 cm.)
Provenance: Richard S. Davis, Minneapolis; M. Knoedler and Co., New York
Exhibitions: Fogg Art Museum, Cambridge, "Twentieth Century Drawings and Watercolors from the Collection of Richard S. Davis," April 20–June 1, 1951 (the drawing then titled *Study for Sacred Fish*); University Art Gallery, University of California, Santa Barbara, "62 Works of Art from Santa Barbara and Vicinity," 1965, No. 57
Literature: University Art Gallery, University of California, *62 Works of Art from Santa Barbara and Vicinity,* Santa Barbara, 1965, No. 57 (ill.)
Lent by Constance McCormick Fearing

Between 1910 and 1918 Giorgio de Chirico produced a number of "metaphysical interiors." As his wife Isabella Far has pointed out, "Time and again he used a room as the setting of his most hallucinatory visions because he liked the security of a room."[1] (Interestingly enough, de Chirico

began his memoirs with the sentence, "My most distant memory is of a big room with a high ceiling."[2]) In these rooms the artist depicted a combination of geometric shapes and seemingly mundane objects such as the fish molds in this drawing. Yet, every object is for de Chirico laden with symbolism. The fish is a traditional symbol of Christianity, and just two years later he was to paint an overtly symbolic fish painting, *Sacred Fish,* in the collection of the Museum of Modern Art, New York. De Chirico conceived of the geometrical figures as symbols of a higher reality. For instance, of the triangle he wrote: "The triangle often arouses in an individual who looks at it, even when he does not know its traditional meaning, a feeling of anxiety and even fear. Thus, rules, squares, and compasses—the tools of geometry—used to haunt and still haunt my mind. I still see them appearing like mysterious stars and rising up behind each of my pictorial creations."[3]

De Chirico was an artist obsessed by materials. On the first page of his memoirs he says: "It is the quality of the material that determines the degree of perfection in a work of art, especially in painting, and this quality is the most difficult thing to understand."[4] Later he recounts that his first drawing teacher "was the first to teach me how to sharpen pencils in a regular way, cutting round the wood with care and symmetry and not in the slovenly manner of many people, making the point of the pencil look like a big toe deformed by cold."[5]

[1]Isabella Far, *de Chirico,* New York, 1968, p. 9.
[2]*The Memoirs of Giorgio de Chirico,* Coral Gables (Florida), 1971, p. 13.
[3]Quoted in Far, *op. cit.,* p. 8.
[4]*Memoirs, op. cit.,* p. 13.
[5]*Ibid.,* p. 21.

JOHN STEUART CURRY
American, 1897–1946

7

Storm Over Lake Otsego, c. 1925 *(ill. p. 112)*
Pencil and watercolor
Signed, bottom right: "John Steuart Curry"
20⅛ x 27⅛ in. (51.1 x 68.8 cm.)
Lent by Mr. and Mrs. George F. McMurray

Curry grew up on a farm in Kansas in a family that was hard-working and deeply religious. From 1921 to 1926 he worked in New York as a rather unsuccessful illustrator. It was during these years that he took frequent painting trips to Cooperstown and Lake Otsego in upper New York State. In 1926 he went to Paris. The years immediately following his return in 1928 were extremely productive ones in which he painted several of his best paintings: *Tornado, Baptism in Kansas, The Gospel Train, Roadworker's Camp,* and *State Fair.*

3 John Steuart Curry, *Storm over Lake Otsego,* 1929, present location unknown

The watercolor *Storm on Lake Otsego* was made just before his European departure, and the large oil based upon it (fig. 3) was to follow in 1929. The storm scene with lightning scaring the horses is typical of Curry's interest in dramatic natural events. His mother once remarked: "As a child John was terribly afraid of thunderstorms. I wonder why he paints so many of them. Perhaps he feels something sublime in their terrific power."[1] Moreover, Curry had frequently sketched horses from his earliest days as an artist on the farm.

The changes occurring between the watercolor and the painting are small but significant, all leading to a concentration in the drama of man, horse, and nature. In the painting the barking dog has been removed; the landscape at the lower right has been simplified; and the lightning has been placed behind the hills in the background.

[1]Quoted in Laurence E. Schmeckebier, *John Steuart Curry's Pageant of America,* New York, 1943, p. 12.

SALVADOR DALI
Spanish, b. 1904

8

Grotesque Heads, c. 1936 (ill. p. 111)
Pen and ink
Signed, bottom right: "Salvador Dali"
16³/₁₆ x 20¹¹/₁₆ in. (41.1 x 52.5 cm.)
Provenance: Clifford Odets
Lent by the Grunwald Center for the Graphic Arts, University of California, Los Angeles

In 1929 Dali became associated with the Surrealist movement in Paris and in that year produced a remarkable series of small paintings which incorporated Freudian dream imagery. The years 1932 to 1936 were the most prolific of his career but ended in his final and vituperative break with the Surrealist movement.

Grotesque Heads is a compendium of the familiar motifs which appear in Dali's paintings of the early 1930s. The grotesque heads occur in *The Invisible Man* and *Imperial Monument to the Child-Woman*; the nude women are similar to those in *The Invisible Man* and to those in the preparatory drawing for the painting, as well as to the woman in the drawing *Andromeda* in the Albright-Knox Gallery; and the fighting men are similar to a preparatory drawing *Figures after William Tell* of c. 1932.[1]

Like many of Dali's drawings of the early 1930s, *Grotesque Heads* is characterized by pure, lyrical, unbroken lines. Little shading is used. By 1937 his drawings employ more shading, and the lines have become short and broken.

[1]All but the last are illustrated in A. Reynolds Morse, *Salvador Dali, 1910–1965,* Greenwich (Conn.), 1965; the *Figures after William Tell* is illustrated in A. Reynolds Morse, *A New Introduction to Salvador Dali,* Cleveland, 1960, p. 65.

WILLEM de KOONING
Dutch/American, b. 1904

9

Woman, 1952 (ill. p. 128)
Pastel, pencil, and charcoal
Signed, bottom right, in pencil: "de Kooning"
14 x 12³/₈ in. (35.6 x 31.4 cm.)
Provenance: Fourcarde-Droll, Inc., New York
Exhibitions: Walker Art Center, Minneapolis, "De Kooning Drawing and Sculpture," 1974, No. 64, circulated to the National Gallery of Canada (Ottawa), Philips Gallery, Albright-Knox Gallery, Museum of Fine Arts (Houston), 1974–1975
Literature: Walker Art Center, *De Kooning Drawing and Sculpture,* Minneapolis, 1974, No. 64 (ill.); Stephanie Barron, "de Kooning's Woman, ca. 1952, A Drawing Recently Acquired by the Museum," *Los Angeles County Museum of Art Bulletin,* 1976, Vol. XXII, pp. 66–72 (ill.)
Lent by the Los Angeles County Museum of Art, Museum Purchase

In the early 1940s de Kooning, who had come to America in 1924, was producing non-objective abstract paintings. It was in these years also that he did his first major paintings of women, a theme to which he returned with great gusto in 1950. For five years he devoted himself to his remarkable series of women. *Woman I,* with which he struggled from 1950 to 1952, caused a great scandal in the art world when it was first exhibited. What did this ugly goddess—a pinup of the 1940s tranformed—mean? She was soon followed by a whole series of women; de Kooning innocently said that he thought of them "as characters in a Gertrude Stein novel, chatting away a mile a minute, most in harmless inanities."[1]

De Kooning's drawings are working drawings, for few of them were created as independent works of art. They are often "exercises in spontaneity—a casting around for images—done in a state of expectant relaxation."[2]

In the summer of 1952, just after he had completed *Woman I*, de Kooning produced a large number of pastel drawings of women. He was at that time working in Southampton, Long Island, and had no studio in which to paint.

[1]Quoted in Thomas B. Hess, *Willem de Kooning Drawings*, Greenwich (Conn.), 1972, p. 41.
[2]*Ibid.*, p. 41.

CHARLES DEMUTH
American, 1883–1935

10

Sailboats (The Love Letter), 1919 *(ill. p. 91)*
Tempera
Signed in pencil, bottom left: "C. Demuth"
15½ x 19⅜ in. (39.4 x 49.3 cm.)
Provenance: Wright Ludington
Exhibitions: American Federation of Art, "Pioneers of Abstract Art in America," 1955–1956; Pomona College, Exhibition of the Stieglitz Circle, 1958; William Penn Memorial Museum, "Charles Demuth of Lancaster," 1966; Municipal Art Gallery of Los Angeles, "Cubism, Its Impact in the U.S.A. 1910–1930," 1967; The Akron Art Institute, "Charles Demuth 1883–1935," 1968; Tacoma Art Center, opening of the new building, 1971; The Civic Art Gallery, Walnut Creek; The Art Galleries, University of California, Santa Barbara, "Charles Demuth, The Mechanical Encrusted on the Living," October 5–November 14, 1971, circulated to the University of California Art Museum (Berkeley), The Philips Collection, Munson-Williams-Proctor Institute, 1971–1972
Literature: Andrew Carnduff Ritchie, *Charles Demuth*, Museum of Modern Art, New York, 1950, p. 67 (ill.); The Akron Art Institute, *Charles Demuth 1883–1935*, 1968, No. 69; The Pennsylvania State University, *Charles Demuth of Lancaster*, 1966, No. 78; American Federation of Arts, *Pioneers of American Abstract Art*, 1955; David Gebhard and Phyllis Plous, *Charles Demuth, The Mechanical Encrusted on the Living*, University of California, Santa Barbara, 1971 (Pl. 73)
Lent by the Santa Barbara Museum of Art, Gift of Wright S. Ludington (45.6.5)

In 1914 Demuth, just back from two years in Europe, spent the summer in Provincetown. It was during this visit that he became knowledgeable about the masts and riggings of small sailboats.

During the winter of 1917–1918 which he spent in Bermuda, he experimented with the advances of both Cubism and Futurism, movements he had closely observed in his years in Paris. In these Bermuda works he composed simplified and stylized arrangements of forms and began to employ the ray lines of Futurism to indicate directional movement much as Feininger was doing at the same time in Germany.

In 1919 Demuth began to work both in tempera and oil. *Sailboats* is typical of these early temperas in its emphasis on strong verticals and in the use of smaller planes, all within a very shallow space. There is a remarkable plastic strength— the sails are almost like architecture—and, the existence of this quality within a classic order has been aptly termed "Cubist-Realism" by Milton Brown.[1]

[1]"Cubist-Realism, an American Style," *Marsyas*, III (1946), p. 147.

11

Lilacs in a Vase, c. 1925 *(ill. p. 93)*
Pencil and watercolor
18 x 12 in. (45.7 x 30.5 cm.)
Provenance: James Graham Gallery, New York
Literature: James K. Ballinger, *Arizona Republic*, Phoenix August 3, 1975 (ill.)
Lent by the Fine Arts Gallery of San Diego

In the 1920s Demuth was one of the artists championed by Alfred Steiglitz in his Gallery 21. Known as the Precisionists, the group included Georgia O'Keeffe and Charles Sheeler.

Demuth's flower watercolors have always been among his most popular works. *Lilacs in a Vase* from around 1925 shows several typical aspects of his watercolor style. There is a careful balancing of the original pencil drawing and the areas of watercolor. Demuth also blots the soft pastel color immediately after applying it to the paper so that it is like a thin veil of color. This is then covered by another layer of either the same or another color. The resulting softness of color and contour is eminently suited to this portrayal of pink and lavender lilac blooms.

RICHARD DIEBENKORN
American, b. 1922

12

Seated Nude, 1960 *(ill. p. 131)*
Pen and ink
Signed, bottom left: "RD 60"
17 x 12½ in. (43.2 x 31.7 cm.)
Lent by Mr. and Mrs. William Brice

Richard Diebenkorn abandoned the emotional Berkeley abstractions, which had gained him his first fame, in 1955, and for over a decade he returned to representational painting. He again turned to abstraction in 1967 when he began his Ocean Park series.

Diebenkorn is one of the most distinguished figurative draftsmen of the past thirty years. His drawings are frequently of individual figures with no background setting. From these drawings he extracts essentials—a gesture, perhaps—which he then synthetically "assembled in a vision in which he achieves an integration of the figure with the environment."[1]

[1]Gerald Nordland, "The Figurative Works of Richard Diebenkorn," *Richard Diebenkorn, Paintings and Drawings, 1943–1976,* Albright-Knox Art Gallery, Buffalo, 1976, p. 30.

ARTHUR DOVE
American, 1880–1946

13

Out the Window, c. 1940 (ill. p. 114)
Watercolor
Signed, bottom center: "Dove"
5 x 7 in. (12.7 x 17.8 cm.)
Provenance: Downtown Gallery, New York
Exhibitions: The Sheldon Memorial Art Gallery of the University of Nebraska, "The Howard S. Wilson Memorial Collection," October 11–November 13, 1966
Literature: The Sheldon Memorial Art Gallery, the University of Nebraska, *The Howard S. Wilson Memorial Collection,* 1966, No. 15 (ill.)
Lent by Louise Wilson Warren

Arthur Dove returned to the United States in 1938 after five years in Europe. He soon settled in Centerport, Long Island, in a former post office right on the Sound. In the next year he suffered a massive heart attack and for the rest of his life remained in bad health.

Out the Window is a work produced during the first year of his recovery when he was allowed to paint for only a short time each day. It represents the view afforded from a window of his house of the lighthouse at the point at the end of the Sound.

The scene represented here is more recognizable than in many of his late landscapes, but it is, nevertheless, marked by Dove's tendency to keep the activity on the surface of the paper and to avoid a sense of spatial perspective. The entire surface is activated by the application of colors of equal intensities.

14

Centerport Series, #2, c. 1941 (ill. p. 114)
Watercolor
Signed, bottom center: "Dove"

5 x 7 in. (12.7 x 17.8 cm.)
Provenance: Downtown Gallery, New York
Exhibitions: The Sheldon Memorial Art Gallery of the University of Nebraska, "The Howard S. Wilson Memorial Collection," October 11–November 13, 1966
Literature: The Sheldon Memorial Art Gallery, the University of Nebraska, *The Howard S. Wilson Memorial Collection,* 1966, No. 16 (ill.)
Lent by Louise Wilson Warren

Dove believed that every object had within it "force lines" or "growth lines." These are not the outlines of the object but forms which reveal the inner forces or tensions inherent in it. In this work, the strong froglike form in the center of the watercolor serves this function. Dove also felt that all things had individual "conditions of light." Of these he wrote: "...There was a long period of searching for something in color which I then called 'conditions of light.' It applied to all objects in nature, flowers, trees, people, apples, cows. These all have their certain condition of light, which establishes them to the eye, to each other, and to the understanding."[1]

[1]Quoted in Barbara Haskell, *Arthur Dove,* San Francisco Museum of Art, 1974, p. 7.

JACOB EPSTEIN
American/English, 1880–1959

15

Head of a Negress, c. 1925 (ill. p. 86)
Pencil
Signed, bottom left: "Epstein"
14⅝ x 21¼ in. (37.8 x 54 cm.)
Provenance: Dalzell Hatfield Galleries, Los Angeles
Literature: Lady Epstein, *Epstein Drawings,* London, 1962, No. 43 (ill.)
Lent by Mr. Jack Willis

Throughout his career the sculptor Jacob Epstein, who settled in London in 1905, was fascinated by exotic women. In the 1920s his two favorite models were the Indians, Sumita and Miriam Patel, who lived with the Epsteins. There are also drawings of Zeda, a flamboyant Turkish model, and a whole series of nude drawings of black women. These nude studies, mainly drawn in the summer of 1928, were reproduced in the book *75 Drawings,* published in 1929.

The Head of a Negress was drawn earlier than the recumbent nudes of 1928. The sitter was probably a member of the cast of the American revue *Blackbirds,* starring Daisy Dunn, which took London by storm in 1925. This revue, the first musical show with an all black cast, seemed in its vitality to epitomize jazz music.

MAX ERNST
German, 1891–1976

16

Two Doves, 1927 (ill. p. 100)
Watercolor, oil, and crayon
Signed and dated, bottom right: "Max Ernst 1927"
$11^{13}/_{16}$ x $9^{13}/_{16}$ in. (30 x 25 cm.)
Provenance: Gift of the artist
Lent by Mrs. Barbara R. Poe

In 1925, one year after the beginning of the Surrealist movement, Max Ernst discovered *frottage*, a process which was the "true equivalent of what had already been known as automatic writing."[1]

> ...I was struck by the obsession imposed upon my excited gaze by the wooden floor, the grain of which had been deepened and exposed by countless scrubbings. I decided to explore the hidden symbolism of this obsession, and to aid my meditative and hallucinatory powers, I derived from the floorboards a series of drawings by dropping pieces of paper on them at random and then rubbing them with black lead....
> The drawings thus obtained steadily lost the character ...of the wood, thanks to a series of suggestions and transmutations that occurred to me spontaneously (as in hypnagogic visions), and assumed the aspect of unbelievably clear images probably revealing the original cause of my obsession....
>
> I marveled at the results and, my curiosity awakened, I was led to examine in the same way all sorts of materials that I happened upon: leaves and their veins, the ragged edges of sackcloth, the palette knife markings on a "modern" painting, and so forth....[2]

The style of *Two Doves* is similar to many of the other *frottages* with its emphasis on the wood grain, its near absence of modeling, and its very shallow space. The content, birds, was one of Ernst's favorite themes during these years when he produced at least two major paintings devoted to doves—*10,000 Doves* of 1925 and *Blue and Rose Doves* of 1926—as well as many paintings and drawings.

[1]Quoted in William S. Rubin, *Dada, Surrealism and their Heritage*, Museum of Modern Art, New York, 1968, p. 82.
[2]*Ibid.*, p. 82.

LYONEL FEININGER
American, 1871–1956

17

Vollersroda, 1918 (ill. p. 78)
Pen and ink, and wash
Signed, bottom left: "Feininger"; Titled, center bottom: "Vollersroda"; Dated, bottom right: "Sonntag d. 6 Jan. 1918"
$7^{7}/_{8}$ x $9^{7}/_{8}$ in. (20 x 25.1 cm.)
Exhibitions: Los Angeles County Museum of Art, "The Cubist Epoch," 1970, No. 86
Literature: Los Angeles County Museum of Art, *Drawings in the Collection of the Los Angeles County Museum of Art*, 1970 (ill., n.p.); Douglas Cooper, *The Cubist Epoch*, Los Angeles County Museum of Art, 1970, (Pl. 140)
Lent by the Los Angeles County Museum of Art, Museum Purchase with Graphic Art Council Funds

Feininger, like Klee and Kandinsky, was a musician and went to Germany in 1887 to study music in Hamburg. He soon became an artist and in the first decade of this century was a highly successful cartoonist ("Wee Willie Winkle's World").

As early as 1907 Feininger wrote, "I visualize quite different values of light form—different possibilities of translation than heretofore—but it seems nearly impossible to free oneself from the accepted reality of nature. That which is seen optically has to go through the process of transformation and crystalization to become a picture."[1]

By the mid-teens his vision had matured, nurtured partly by Futurism and its interest in achieving a sense of rapid movement through the use of "ray lines." Walter Gropius, who asked Feininger to join the faculty of the Bauhaus, commented on Feininger's use of line: "I don't believe Feininger thinks or builds in terms of architecture. These straight lines are rays. They are not architectural, they are optical."[2]

Vollersroda is one of Feininger's most successful pen and ink drawings. More dense than many, it fractures the church building into planes with little sense of three-dimensionality. The lines create an optical interaction among the church, the surrounding buildings, and the sky with its swirling clouds.

Vollersroda was a small town near Weimar which Feininger used to visit during day excursions. He treated the same subject at least four other times.[3]

[1]Quoted in Peter Selz, *German Expressionist Painting*, Berkeley, 1957, p. 279.
[2]*The Work of Lyonel Feininger*, Cleveland Museum of Art, 1951, p. 13.
[3]The first is a woodcut of 1919, illustrated in L. E. Prasse, *Lyonel Feininger*, Cleveland Museum of Art, 1972, p. 203. Three paintings of Vollersroda exist: numbers 206 and 373 in Hans Hesse, *Lyonel Feininger*, New York, 1961, pp. 267 and 283 and number 140 in *Lyonel Feininger*, Haus der Kunst, Munich, 1973.

4 Albert Gleizes, *Composition with Two Nudes*, c. 1922, present location
unknown

SAM FRANCIS
American, b. 1923

18

Untitled, 1955 (ill. p. 124)
Watercolor
Signed and dated on reverse
13¼ x 9½ in. (33.7 x 24.2 cm.)
Provenance: Gimpel Fils, London; Colonel Davis Collec-
tion; Redfern Gallery, London; Stephen Hahn Gallery, New
York; Margo Leavin Gallery, Los Angeles
Exhibitions: Gimpel Fils, London, "Sam Francis Exhibi-
tion," May 1957, No. 20
Lent by Douglas S. Cramer

Among the Abstract Expressionists of the early 1950s it was
Sam Francis who, along with Mark Rothko, concentrated
most intently on color as subject. Francis has said that one
of the crucial events in his development as an artist occurred
while he was recuperating in a hospital from a war wound.
What began to fascinate him was the quality of light—"not
just the play of light but the substance of which light is
made."[1] And, this is color. Soon revealed in his work also
was his interest in the "rich vocabulary of ever-shifting
cloud forms."[2]

His paintings and watercolors of the early 1950s are made
up of webs of color cells which create a sense of space
and depth. Like the light effects in the paintings of Claude
Lorrain, there is a sense in Francis' watercolors of light
flowing forward from the inner depth of the work and creating screens of color. By 1955 the color cells begin to break
apart and the forms to loosen. Francis' use of dripped paint
and free gesture reveals his affinity to other Abstract Expressionists.

[1]James Johnson Sweeney, *Sam Francis,* Museum of Fine Arts,
Houston, 1972, p. 16.
[2]*Ibid.,* p. 16.

ALBERT GLEIZES
French, 1881–1953

19

Composition with Two Nudes, 1920 (ill. p. 81)
Pencil and watercolor
Signed and dated, bottom right: "Alb. Gleizes 20"
7⅞ x 5⅞ in. (20 x 14.9 cm.)
Lent by Mr. and Mrs. Charles E. Ducommun

By 1920 Cubism was virtually dead, having been replaced
by the audacious work of the Dadaists. Gleizes, however,
was one of the few artists to remain a Cubist and, in fact,
continued to be one until his death.

In the early 1920s Gleizes codified his theories and incorporated them into his book *Kubismus* of 1928. In it he called
the tilting planes "translations" and the circular movements
"rotations." As Daniel Robbins has pointed out in discus-
sing the large painting (fig. 4) Gleizes developed from this
hitherto unpublished watercolor: "In order to achieve what
he called 'supple movement,' Gleizes organized his canvas
by the guided movement of a chosen plane surface. Plane
surfaces move back and forth, to right and left, progressing
to more complex forms, so that curves were infused into the
developing rhythm."[1]

[1]*Albert Gleizes,* Solomon R. Guggenheim Museum, New
York, 1964, p. 77.

JULIO GONZALES
Spanish, 1876–1942

20

Study for a Sculpture, 1941 (ill. p. 116)
Pencil, pen and ink, and watercolor
Initialed and dated, bottom right: "J.G., 26-2-41"
9¾ x 6⅜ in. (24.8 x 16.2 cm.)
Provenance: Galerie Chalette, New York
Exhibitions: Galerie Chalette, New York, "Julio Gonzales,"
1961, No. 101
Lent by Mr. and Mrs. Philip Gersh

After years of inactivity as an artist, Julio Gonzales began to make sculpture in the 1930s after Picasso, a long-time friend, asked him to collaborate with him on several sculptures. In his first work of the 1930s he used flat sheets of iron which he cut and incised with outlines of figures or heads. These read more as drawings than sculpture. His later advances in open-form sculpture were to have a strong influence on David Smith in America and Butler and Chadwick in England.

During the opening years of World War II Gonzales could no longer weld his favorite iron because of the scarcity of oxygen and acetylene. In consequence, he had to resort to drawings, such as this one, or to modeling in plaster. Like all of his sculpture, the project indicated in this drawing is of a human figure, a subject which Gonzales often treated with real wit.

ARSHILE GORKY
Russian/American, 1905–1948

21

Study for Nighttime, Enigma and Nostalgia, 1931–1932
(ill. p. 115)
Pencil, pen and ink
Signed, in pencil, top right: "Gorky"
12¾ x 21¾ in. (32.4 x 55.2 cm.)
Provenance: Allan Stone Gallery, New York
Exhibitions: Museum of Modern Art, New York, "Arshile Gorky: Painting, Drawings, and Studies," December 17–February 12, 1963, circulated to Washington Gallery of Modern Art, 1963; M. Knoedler and Co., New York, November 25–December 27, 1969
Literature: William C. Seitz, *Arshile Gorky: Painting, Drawings, Studies,* Museum of Modern Art, New York, 1963, p. 20 (ill.); Julien Levy, *Arshile Gorky,* New York, 1966, Pl. 63 (ill.)
Lent by Mr. and Mrs. Philip Gersh

In the drawings of 1931–1932, Gorky was responding to the surrealist images and poetic linear shapes of Joan Miro, whose work he knew from exhibitions in New York, and to Cubism, which was still popular in the city at that time. His Cubist vocabulary is evident in the "architectonic setting and placement, and an interlocked complex of curved shapes that resemble an artist's palette with its eye-like perforation, or the patterns that in cubist still life function as shadows, or represent bowls, musical instruments and gourds."[1]

One of the major paintings of the early 1930s was *Nighttime, Enigma and Nostalgia* for which Gorky made a number of preliminary drawings. The earliest is a pure line drawing (fig. 5) which is marked by the clarity of the curving shapes. The addition of shading in the Gersh's drawing gives a new resonance and richness to the forms and a sense

5 Arshile Gorky, *Study for Nighttime, Enigma and Nostalgia,* pencil, 1931–1932, Museum of Modern Art, New York, Gift of Richard S. Zeisler

of mystery to the image. This richness is intensified by the density of the blacks, resulting from Gorky's technique of wetting some of the ink passages. In the painting this density is achieved by the sheer thickness of the impasto.

[1]William Chapin Seitz, *Arshile Gorky: Paintings, Drawings, Studies,* Museum of Modern Art, New York, 1962, p. 20.

22

Study for Liver is the Cock's Comb, 1943 (ill. p. 122)
Ink, crayon, and pencil
Signed and dated, bottom right: "A. Gorky 43"
19 x 25½ in. (48.2 x 64.7 cm.)
Provenance: Julien Levy; Mrs. Mougouche Philips, England
Exhibitions: Everett Ellin Gallery, Los Angeles, "Arshile Gorky: Forty Drawings 1929–1947," April 9–May 5, 1962; Museum of Modern Art, New York, "Arshile Gorky: Paintings, Drawings, and Studies," December 17–February 12, 1963, circulated to Washington Gallery of Modern Art; The Arts Council of Great Britain, The Tate Gallery, London, April 1–May 2, 1965, circulated to Palais des Beaux Arts, Brussels, and Museum Boymans-Van-Beuningen, Rotterdam, 1965
Literature: Ethel K. Schwabacher, *Arshile Gorky,* New York, 1957, No. 38 (ill.); William C. Seitz, *Arshile Gorky: Paintings, Drawings, and Studies,* Museum of Modern Art, New York, 1963; Julien Levy, *Arshile Gorky,* New York, 1966, Pl. 6 (ill.); Barbara Rose, *American Art Since 1900,* New York, 1975, p. 145 (ill.)
Lent by The Weisman Collection of Art

The summer of 1943 marked a decisive turning point in Gorky's career. During a visit to his parents' farm in Virginia, he produced scores of drawings in pencil and colored crayon—lyrical explosions which mark his free response to nature. Ethel Schwabacher, in a rather lyrical style of her own, describes these responses:

Sitting before nature, Gorky dissected root, stem, insect, leaf and flower, studying genesis and process. ...He concentrated on the image of flight as action, fecund, hedonistic...further, the stiff core of the waving pliant grasses interested him; he translated this stiffness as bone, contrasting the stasis of bone with the metamorphosis of the leaf....images disentangled from the mesh of outward appearances variously and provocatively repeat the sexual theme; in the boot shape, fetishistic symbol for women; in flowers which suggest flight or imprecation; and in the cinglet, through which amoebic shapes push up to birth.[1]

From the natural facts he observed, Gorky created his own idiom of what André Breton has called "hybrid forms." These symbolic forms ushered in Gorky's mature style and appeared in his paintings only a year later. The painting *Liver is the Cock's Comb* of 1944 is in the Albright-Knox Gallery.

[1]Ethel K. Schwabacher, *Arshile Gorky,* Whitney Museum of American Art, New York, 1957, pp. 97–98.

GEORGE GROSZ
German/American, 1893–1959

23
_____

Broadway, 1934 (*ill. p. 105*)
Watercolor
Signed, bottom right: "Grosz"
24¾ x 17 in. (60.3 x 43.2 cm.)
Provenance: David B. Findlay, Inc., New York
Exhibitions: Galerie Claude Bernard, Paris, February 1966; Fine Arts Gallery of San Diego, "20 Century Tempo," June–August 1968; Fine Arts Gallery of San Diego, "20th Century Art," July–September 1970
Literature: Galerie Claude Bernard, *George Grosz Dessins et Aquarelles,* Paris, 1966 (ill.)
Anonymous Loan

George Grosz visited New York for six months in 1932. In January 1933, a few weeks before Hitler would have had all his work confiscated, he and his family immigrated to the United States. In a letter to a friend, Grosz recorded his impressions of New York City where they settled: "New York—that great, wonderful city. I love this town. I have seen tramps sleeping on newspapers in Union Square...I have seen Negroes, Chinese, red-haired Irishmen, sailors; Broadway aglow at night; the huge department stores; workers in overalls suspended between steel girders...Wall Street and shouting brokers at the stock exchange...I have seen obscene shows, where sweet girls stripped to the applause of men...this town is full of pictures and contrasts..."[1]

This welter of impressions found an outlet in the large number of watercolors Grosz produced. In his autobiog-

6 Philip Guston, *Room 1,* 1954–1955, Los Angeles County Museum of Art, Purchased with funds from the Contemporary Art Council

raphy he wrote of these early New York years: "Evenings, after I had returned home from my classes, I let the watercolors run over my paper as I excitedly painted my impressions of the day. The city was charged with stimuli for me and I was filled with inner fire and receptivity."[2]

In 1933 he produced at least sixty large watercolors. For the most part they are reasonably factual observations. In the next year his pessimistic, satiric vision asserted itself anew. He wrote: "The world is so full of grotesques and hellish happenings, that one can hardly make a joke. Everything fire-red, blood-red, black and profanely dark, and this bloody pastry is served with stinking mustard. That is where laughter ceases."[3]

Broadway is one of the most apocalyptic of his New York watercolors. It is like a glowing illustration of the City of Dreadful Night in which spectral beings appear to float like figures in a nightmare, eyes become sockets in a skull, and veins become visible beneath the yellowed skin.

[1]Quoted in Hans Hess, *George Grosz,* London, 1974, pp. 175–176.
[2]*Ibid.,* p. 270.
[3]*Ibid.,* p. 185.

PHILIP GUSTON
American, b. 1913

24

Untitled, 1954 (ill. p. 128)
Brush and black ink
Signed and dated, bottom right: "P. Guston 1954"
18 x 23⅛ in. (45.7 x 59 cm.)
Provenance: Adler Gallery, Beverly Hills
Lent by Mr. Robert H. Halff and Mr. Carl W. Johnson

Philip Guston, who grew up in Los Angeles, achieved success as a figurative painter in the 1940s. In 1947 he abandoned this mode to become an abstractionist.

1954, the year of this untitled drawing, was an important year of transition in his career. He started and destroyed many paintings and produced a large number of drawings. Until 1954 he had continued to do figure drawings, but these ceased in 1954 and in the following four years he produced very few drawings of any kind.

The relationship of Guston's drawings and paintings is close as we can see by comparing this drawing to *Room I* in the Los Angeles County Museum (fig. 6). In the drawing he was "experimenting with the creation of masses without contour, as in the painting he increasingly began to experiment with black as a color."[1] In the painting, however, he is moving from the denseness of the center outward, while in the drawing he is moving downward, like a rhythmic cascade.

[1]H. H. Arnasson, *Philip Guston,* Solomon R. Guggenheim Museum, New York, 1962, p. 29.

ERICH HECKEL
German, 1883–1970

25

Kneeling Nude Woman, 1913 (ill. p. 73)
Pencil and watercolor
Signed and dated, bottom right: "Erich Heckel 13"
20 x 16 in. (50.8 x 40.6 cm.)
Provenance: Felix Landau Gallery, Los Angeles, 1966
Exhibitions: La Jolla Museum of Contemporary Art, "The Kondon Collection," December 19, 1975–February 1, 1976.
Lent by Dr. Vance E. Kondon

Erich Heckel was the mediator in the *Brücke* group, first in Dresden, later in Berlin. He managed to hold them—or a few of them—together until 1913, the year of this drawing.

It was he, too, who organized their affairs, including arranging exhibitions and the publication of their portfolios.

Along with Kirchner, Pechstein, and Mueller, Heckel spent the summers at the seaside. In Dresden the group went to the Moritzberger Sea and from Berlin to the West and North Seas—to Fehman, Prerow, Nidden, and Dangast. There they drew and painted nudes in the open air as if they were symbols of their liberated life—free both from society's constraints and from the iron grip of artistic tradition and academic training.

Close to this work in conception and style is the drawing and watercolor *Yellow Nude* of 1912.[1] In both drawings the artist has used a schematized setting for the study of the nude, voluptuous woman; in both there are simple sails for boats, a triangular tree(?) behind the figure, a tree and branch at the left, and reflected shapes on the sand.

[1]Illustrated in *Die Kunstlergruppe Brücke und der deutsche Expressionismus, Sammlung Buchheim,* Stadtische Galerie im Lenbachhaus, Munich, 1973, No. 10.

HANS HOFMANN
German/American, 1880–1966

26

Untitled, 1943 (ill. p. 125)
Watercolor, pen and ink
Signed and dated, bottom right: "1 H. 26 43. HaH"
17¾ x 23¾ in. (45 x 60.3 cm.)
Provenance: André Emmerich, New York
Lent by Maybelle Bayly Wolfe

Hans Hofmann was one of the great teachers of the twentieth century. In the 1920s when he was in Munich, American students sought him out, and as a result of these associations, he was invited to teach at the University of California, Berkeley, in the summer of 1930. He returned to Berkeley in 1931, remained in the United States, and then opened a school in New York City.

His paintings and watercolors of the early 1940s are dominated by his wonderful line, with color still serving as an adjunct to the linear forms. The lines serve to contain a plane or painted areas; "as outline it divides and combines; as an aesthetic carrier it flows and becomes the vehicle of free, searching effects."[1]

[1]Quoted in William Seitz, *Hans Hofmann,* Museum of Modern Art, New York, 1963, p. 24.

AUGUSTUS JOHN
English, 1878–1961

27

Seated Nude, c. 1923 (ill. p. 89)
Pencil
16¾ x 11⅓ in. (42.5 x 28.8 cm.)
Provenance: Dalzell Hatfield Galleries, Los Angeles
Lent by Mr. Jack Willis

Augustus John was the most fashionable English portrait painter of the first half of this century. Early in his career he had shown real promise as an artist, but this promise was never fully realized. His *Portrait of Mme. Suggia,* finished in 1923, "must be accounted the last late masterpiece of John's professional career."[1] It was around that year that John made this pencil study of a nude woman with her toussled, fashionably short hair.[2]

John had been taught to draw using charcoal at the Slade School in London. But, prior to his training he had used pencil, and it was pencil that later became his favorite medium.

The drawing combines an elegance of line—concomitant with the elegance of the pose and the thin hands—with a freedom in the oblique-stroke shading. Particularly striking are the aristocratic hand with its crooked little finger and the strong thin line of the woman's left side which delineates the pudgy abdomen and seems at the same time to support the tiny bosom.

[1]Malcolm Easton and Michael Holroyd, *The Art of Augustus John,* Boston, 1975, p. 27.
[2]For similar drawings of 1923 see *European Drawings in the Collection of the Santa Barbara Museum of Art,* Alfred Moir ed., Santa Barbara, 1976, pp. 137–140.

ERNST LUDWIG KIRCHNER
German, 1880–1938

28

Man and Woman, c. 1908 (ill. p. 72)
Colored crayon
Verso: Estate seal
13 x 18 in. (33 x 45.7 cm.)
Provenance: Nierdorf Gallery, Berlin
Exhibitions: La Jolla Museum of Contemporary Art, "The Kondon Collection," December 19, 1975–February 1, 1976
Lent by Dr. Vance E. Kondon

Like so many other artists active in the first decade of the twentieth century, Kirchner, during his years in Dresden as a member of the *Brücke* group, was struggling with a basic artistic problem: the inconsistency of producing a three-dimensional image on a flat surface. That his style became increasingly two-dimensional can perhaps be best traced in his many rapid sketches from nature. In these works he developed appropriate linear and planar abbreviations which he called "hieroglyphs." Thus, in *Man and Woman* Kirchner placed the man almost directly above, rather than behind the woman and distorted the background to de-emphasize depth. Similarly, his use of colors—for example the greens of the foreground and background—create a decorative pattern which works against a sense of depth.

This drawing is related to two other works of 1908, both of prone figures: the three-colored lithograph *Man Lying on the Beach* and the drawing *Lying Pair in the Fresh Air.*[1]

[1]The latter is illustrated in *E. L. Kirchner Aquarelle, Pastelle, Handzeichnungen,* Galerie Meta Nierendorf, Berlin, 1963, No. 81.

PAUL KLEE
Swiss, 1879–1940

29

Bunt Fenestes an der Lage gemessen, (Stained-Glass Windows in a Precise Position), 1928 (ill. p. 98)
Pencil, ink, and watercolor
Signed, bottom left: "Klee"; Titled, bottom right: "Bunt Fenestes an der Lage gemessen"; Dated, bottom left: "1928 V.1"
6 x 18⅜ in. (15.2 x 46.6 cm.)
Provenance: Purchased from the artist in 1928
Lent by Herbert and Joella Bayer

Klee began his *Creative Credo* of 1920 with the statement "Art does not reproduce the visual but makes visible." The artist, according to Klee, is one who looks beyond the surface and in the process of creation makes underlying truths visible. That the final image—the art—does not look like the source was beautifully explained by Klee in a metaphor of a tree. Reality is the roots; the artist is the trunk; and the art is the leaves. No one should expect leaves to look like roots.

Klee had begun his career as a draftsman. (He did not begin to paint until 1919.) His eleven years as a master at the Bauhaus (1921–1932) were perhaps the most productive of his life. They were the years when he felt in strong communication with a power beyond himself, the true source of his inspiration. He wrote of this source: "My hand wholly the instrument of some remote power. It is not my intellect that runs the show, but something different, something higher and more distant—somewhere else. I must have great friends there, bright ones, but somber ones too."[1]

Stained-Glass Windows in a Precise Position, a work of 1928, closely balances forces in its basic two-part composition. It is less detailed and more abstract than many of Klee's works. In it he has pasted together two sheets of paper and has balanced shapes asymmetrically across the division.

[1]Quoted in Will Grohmann, *Paul Klee Drawings,* New York, 1960, p. 17.

30

Scheren-gitter und seine Feindin, (Rail Fence and His Enemy), 1940 (ill. p. 99)
Brush and paste color
Signed, bottom left: "Paul Klee"; Titled and dated, bottom right: "Scheren-gitter und seine Feindin, 1940"
8¼ x 13¾ in. (21 x 24.9 cm.)
Provenance: Curt Valentin, New York
Exhibitions: Institute of Contemporary Arts, London, "Fifty Drawings by Paul Klee from the Collection of Curt Valentin," New York, circulated to the Kestner-Gesellschaft, Hannover, 1954, No. 50
Literature: Institute of Contemporary Arts, London, *Fifty Drawings by Paul Klee from the Collection of Curt Valentin*, 1954, No. 5
Anonymous Loan

In the last five months of his life Klee executed 251 drawings. In them and in the works since 1937, when his late style with its powerful, broad brush strokes began, Klee was overtly concerned with man's fate in this world and in the next. Among this last outpouring of 1940 were a series of archetypes and the Passions. In them an urgency of theme meshes with a strong, bold, and very direct style.

A similar drawing of this year *Die Schlangengöttin und ihr Fein (The Snakegoddess and her Foe)* shows a snake and a lattice-like dog also observed by a smiling face at the top.[1]

[1]Illustrated in *Paul Klee,* Kunsthalle, Basel, 1967, No. 206.

GUSTAV KLIMT
Austrian, 1862–1918

31

Two Standing Female Nudes, c. 1918 (ill. p. 77)
Pencil
Signed, bottom left: "Gustav Klimt"
22½ x 14¾ (57.1 x 37.5 cm.)
Provenance: N. Otto Kallir; St. Etienne Gallery, New York
Exhibitions: La Jolla Museum of Contemporary Art, "The Kondon Collection," December 19, 1975–February 1, 1976
Lent by Dr. Vance E. Kondon

Gustav Klimt grew out of the Art Nouveau movement in Austria. In his elegant paintings he carefully balanced the three-dimensionality of his figures against gorgeously patterned clothes and backgrounds. A similar balancing occurs between two-dimensionality and plasticity in his drawings, even in this late drawing of around 1918. The nude is described in thin, broken lines which create a nervous pattern and which seem to deny the corporality of the bodies. At the same time in a few places—in this instance along the breast and right side of the right hand figure—the repeated lines create a heavy, dark area which emphasizes the volume of the figure. The two models of this drawing were favorites of Klimt's and appear in many of his late drawings.

FRANZ KLINE
American, 1910–1962

32

Untitled, 1947 (ill. p. 125)
Brush and oil
Signed and dated, lower right: "47 Kline"
22½ x 29½ in. (29.2 x 74.9 cm.) (sight)
Provenance: Paul Kantor Gallery, Beverly Hills
Exhibitions: Los Angeles County Museum of Art, "New York School: The First Generation Paintings of the 1940's and 1950's," July 16–August 1, 1965
Literature: Maurice Tuchman, *The New York School,* Los Angeles County Museum of Art, 1965, No. 57 (ill. p. 91)
Lent by Mrs. Nathan Alpers

Kline's paintings of the 1950s, even though they look as if they were created with great ease, were preceded by sketch after sketch. He was a passionate draftsman and in his drawings he attempted to catch an idea or to test a gesture or motion. "Many of the drawings indicated as 'studies' are more properly events preceding or related to a given oil painting or mimetic rehearsals of gesture awaiting their ultimate and ideal scale rather than studies in the traditional sense."[1]

Kline's first significant abstract works date from the period 1945–1947, and they evolved naturally from his preoccupation with the act—the gestures—of drawing. In fact, the story is told that his major change in style was precipitated by an accidental enlargement and projection on the wall of a small drawing of a favorite chair by a Bell-opticon machine. This story is revealing, too, of the quality of monumentality inherent in Kline's more powerful drawings.

In this drawing of 1947 we can see Kline exploring different qualities of line—particularly different widths and the effects which can be achieved when the paint begins to dry on the brush—and of gesture. Also apparent in this work is his ability to create balance in an off-center composition. As Frank O'Hara has pointed out, Kline "had always the draughtsman's gift of placement. Forms, strokes, dots and dabs, found unerringly their ideal position in the space of his surfaces. He was very conscious of this quality, and of the vitality and freshness of a slightly 'off' positioning."[2]

[1]Frank O'Hara, *Franz Kline,* Whitechapel Gallery, London, 1964, p. 8.
[2]*Ibid.,* p. 10.

33

Untitled, 1953 (ill. p. 127)
Brush and black ink
$8^5/_{16}$ x $10^{13}/_{16}$ in. (21.1 x 27.4 cm.)
Provenance: Allan Stone Galleries, New York; E. G. Gallery, Kansas City; Margo Leavin Gallery, Los Angeles
Lent by Councilman Joel Wachs, Los Angeles

In the early 1950s Kline produced a remarkable series of black and white paintings. Like the larger works, the drawings of this period are characterized by broad gestures, often rough and abrupt. These works have frequently been compared with Oriental calligraphy. It has been pointed out, however, that "the strokes and linear gestures of the painter's arm and shoulder are aimed at an ultimate structure of feeling rather than at ideograph or writing. Unlike Tobey, Kline did not find a deep spiritual affinity in Japanese art, beyond his appreciation of its pictorial values and perhaps a fondness for the diagonal and for the build-up of unified imagery through exquisite detail also appreciated fully by so many nineteenth-century European painters."[1]

This drawing reveals Kline's feeling for the edge of the image. There is a sense of a pressure about to explode at the sides, which differs markedly, for instance, from Motherwell's treatment of the edge in *Spanish Elegy* (Cat. No. 53).

[1]Frank O'Hara, *Franz Kline,* Whitechapel Gallery, London, 1964, p. 10.

KÄTHE KOLLWITZ
German, 1867–1945

34

Bust-Length Portrait of a Woman with Folded Arms, 1904
(ill. p. 71)
Crayon and pastel on violet-gray paper
Signed and dated, bottom right: "04 Käthe Kollwitz"
$23^5/_8$ x $15^3/_4$ in. (60 x 40 cm.)
Provenance: Peter Deitsch, New York
Exhibitions: Frederick S. Wight Art Gallery, University of California, Los Angeles, "German Expressionist Art, The Robert Gore Rifkind Collection," February 27–April 17, 1977, No. 16
Literature: Orrel P. Reed, Jr., *German Expressionist Art, The Robert Gore Rifkind Collection,* University of California, Los Angeles, 1977, No. 16 (ill.)
Lent by Gogi Grant Rifkind

7 Käthe Kollwitz, *Halbfigur einer Frau mit verschrankten Armen,* Klipstein 85, two-color lithograph, 1905

Käthe Kollwitz has been movingly described: "This woman with her great heart has taken the people into her mothering arms with somber and tender pity. She is the voice of the silence of the sacrificed."[1] She lived in Berlin with her husband, a doctor who practiced in the slums of the city.

Academically trained in Berlin and Munich, she decided very early in her career that her real talent was in graphics. Although her individual style soon set her apart from the work of academic artists, she did adhere to her academic training by producing a number of preparatory drawings for her prints. This pastel was one of at least five drawings for a print (fig. 7).[2]

Also typical of her training is the use of back-lighting, the effect of which is to throw a strong light upon the right side of the figure and face.[3] The areas of shadow, however, are treated schematically, particularly on the neck and shoulder. The simplification and boldness of this technique heightens the pathos of the woman with her eyes lost in thought, her mouth turned down in sadness, and her hands firmly grasping her bony arms.

[1]Romain Rollands, quoted in Bernard S. Myers, *The German Expressionists, a Generation in Revolt,* New York, 1957, p. 24.
[2]Four others are illustrated in Otto Nagel, *The Drawings of Käthe Kollwitz,* New York, 1972, nos. 364–367.
[3]Orrel P. Reed, Jr., *German Expressionist Art, The Robert Gore Rifkind Collection,* University of California, Los Angeles, 1977, p. 12.

8 Käthe Kollwitz, *Prisoners,* etching, 1908, The Robert Gore Rifkind
   Collection, Los Angeles

Studies of Men, 1908 (ill. p. 70)
Crayon and charcoal
Signed, bottom right: "Kollwitz"
17⅜ x 22⅝ in. (44.8 x 57.4 cm.)
Literature: Orrell P. Reed, Jr., *German Expressionist Art, The
Robert Gore Rifkind Collection,* University of California, Los
Angeles, No. 19 (ill.)
Lent by The Robert Gore Rifkind Collection

It is symptomatic of Kollwitz's empathy for suffering labor-
ers that her first major work (1894–1898) was the series *The
Weavers,* based on the unsuccessful revolt of the weavers
in 1844. Her next series was based on a similar insurrection,
but this time it was the sixteenth-century peasants' revolt.
She worked on this project for six years. *Studies of Men* is one
of at least sixteen preparatory drawings for a print in this
series entitled *Prisoners* (fig. 8).[1] Kollwitz reduced the size of
the forcefully observed figures when working on the final
plate, for the figures in this drawing are larger than those in
the print. Her preparatory drawings are not only detailed
studies of individual figures and parts of bodies but also of
the entire composition (fig. 9). In the print the man's
head is fifth from the left.

O. P. Reed has observed that many of the faces in the print
are of the same model, a common academic practice. However, the effect in the print is that "these are not individuals
as symbols, but masses in revolt. They were the nameless,
not the individualistic. They were from a time grown fluid
in memory, four hundred years before, from history books
made real."[2]

[1] Fifteen are illustrated in Otto Nagel, *The Drawings of Käthe
Kollwitz,* New York, 1972, Nos. 425–438.
[2] Orrel P. Reed, Jr., *German Expressionist Art: The Robert Gore
Rifkind Collection,* University of California, Los Angeles,
1976, p. 13.

FRANTIŠEK KUPKA
Czechoslovakian, 1871–1957

Dynamisme, 1912 (ill. p. 79)
Charcoal and white chalk
Signed, bottom right: "Kupka"
12 x 13¼ in. (30.4 x 33.6 cm.)
Provenance: Robert Elkhorn Gallery, New York
Exhibitions: Robert Elkhorn Gallery, New York, "Twen-
tieth Century Masters," September 27–October 29, 1969,
No. 10
Lent by Mr. and Mrs. M. A. Gribin

Kupka has been identified with Orphic Cubism, the movement which, according to Apollinaire, created art out of

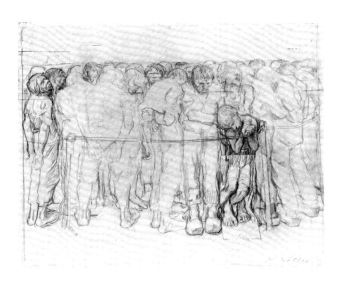

9 Käthe Kollwitz, *The Prisoners,* pencil, Kupferstichkabinett, Kunst-
   museum Basel

10 František Kupka, *Organization of Graphic Motifs I*, 1912–1913, Royal Marks Gallery, New York

elements not borrowed from nature and which "must simultaneously give a pure aesthetic pleasure; a structure which is self-evident; and a sublime meaning, that is, a subject."[1]

Like the Cubist painters, however, Kupka was firmly rooted in nature and saw in natural forms the spiritual reality and cosmic order which govern the universe. His is essentially a spiritual art which grew out of his deep belief in spiritualism (he was a medium for years) and theosophy. It was primarily through rhythm that he attempted to capture the underlying cosmic order. As Margit Rowell has pointed out, for Kupka, "the natural processes of growth, expansion, rotation, dilation, construction are visible inferences of rhythms which man, as a part of the cosmic order, contains within his innermost being. These rhythms provide the structure of the artist's vision."[2]

Dynamisme was produced during Kupka's "heroic years," 1910–1913. It was one of many preliminary drawings and sketches for the painting *Organization of Graphic Motifs I* (fig. 10). In a manuscript of 1912–1913, Kupka wrote extensively of the concept inherent in the painting and its preliminary drawings. It has been summarized by Rowell:

> In our inner visions, fragments of images float before our eyes. In order to capture these fragments, we unconsciously trace lines between them and by thus setting up a network of relationships, we arrive at a coherent whole. These lines drawn to organize our visions are like "stereoscopic bridges" between fragments in space. . . . The lines of this network define points in space and directions. They provide the scaffolding of the image; they capture the rhythmic relationships be-

tween impressions. And this is the real subject of the painter: the lyrical or tragic schema of nature poeticized or dramatized. Details, forms, figures, objects may subsequently be added to articulate the image further."[3]

As was customary with him, Kupka used a natural motif as his starting point; in this case a road between houses in which all but the vertical lines are drawn off into a central vanishing point at the right. In *Dynamisme* we can still see this point at the right, but the center is filled with enigmatic forms which nearly disappear in the final, painted version.

[1] *Les Peintres cubistes,* 1913, English translation by Edward F. Fry, *Cubism,* New York, 1966, p. 117.
[2] Meda Mladek and Margit Rowell, *František Kupka,* Solomon R. Guggenheim Museum, New York, 1975, p. 48.
[3] *Ibid.,* pp. 198–200.

37

Flower, c. 1925 (ill. p. 74)
Watercolor
Signed, bottom right: "Kupka"
9½ x 8¾ in. (24.1 x 22.2 cm.)
Provenance: Rose Fried Gallery, New York
Lent by Mr. David H. Steinmetz

Flower, a work of about 1925, is, like *Dynamisme,* concerned with rhythm. This time the concentric movement inward of the flower petals leads us, as it were, into the heart of nature. It, too, is a preliminary work for a painting.[1]

It is interesting to compare *Flower* to Franz Marc's treatment of a similar theme of a decade earlier (Cat. No. 43). In both cases the artists are concerned with capturing universal order; for both considered art essentially spiritual.

[1] The painting, *Fleur,* is in the Musée National d'Art Moderne, Paris, and is illustrated (No. 91) in D. Fédit, *L'Oeuvre de Kupka,* Musée National d'Art Moderne, 1966.

GASTON LACHAISE
French/American, 1882–1935

38

Standing Nude with Drape, c. 1927 (ill. p. 88)
Pencil and ink
Signed, bottom left: "G. Lachaise"
16¾ x 10 in. (42.5 x 25.4 cm.)
Exhibitions: Los Angeles County Museum of Art, "Gaston Lachaise: Sculpture and Drawing," 1963–1964, No. 127; San Francisco Museum of Modern Art, "An Exhibition of the Sculpture and Drawing of Gaston Lachaise," September 26–October 29, 1967; Herbert F. Johnson Museum of Art,

"Gaston Lachaise," circulated to the Frederick S. Wight Art Gallery, University of California, Los Angeles, Museum of Contemporary Art, Walker Art Center, 1974–1975
Literature: Gerald Nordland, *Gaston Lachaise: Sculpture and Drawing,* Los Angeles County Museum of Art, 1963; San Francisco Museum of Modern Art, *An Exhibition of the Sculpture and Drawing of Gaston Lachaise,* San Francisco, 1967; Herbert F. Johnson Museum of Art, *Gaston Lachaise,* Ithaca, New York, 1974
Lent by Mr. and Mrs. H. M. Rushing

Born in Paris, Lachaise came to the United States in 1906 in pursuit of the married woman with whom he had fallen in love and was later to marry, Isabel Nagle. She became the "spirit" behind his work and was the model for many of his sculptures.

Lachaise's drawings are seldom working drawings related to specific sculptures. Those which are, are clumsily executed and remind one that as a student Lachaise almost failed his drawing course.[1] What Lachaise sought above all in his independent drawings was a sense of spontaneity. And he often succeeded brilliantly, as in this drawing of a woman drying herself. With a very few lines he has captured the twisting movement of the figure, with hip thrown out, torso turned, and large breasts thrust forward. Like most of his women, she is both elegant and highly sensual.

[1]Gerald Nordland, *Gaston Lachaise, Sculpture and Drawings,* Los Angeles County Museum of Art, 1963, not paginated.

RICO LEBRUN
Italian/American, 1900–1964

39

Sunflower, 1947 *(ill. p. 119)*
Pen and ink
Signed, bottom right: "Lebrun 1947"
18⅝ x 24⅜ in. (47.3 x 61.8 cm.)
Exhibitions: Los Angeles County Museum of Art, "Rico Lebrun (1900–1964)," December 5, 1967–January 14, 1968, circulated to Instituto Nacional de Bellas Artes, Mexico, D.F., University of Arizona (Tucson), University of California (Berkeley), Seattle Art Museum; Oklahoma Art Center (Oklahoma City), National Collection of Fine Arts (Washington, D.C.), 1968, No. 79
Literature: Henry J. Seldis, *Rico Lebrun (1900–1964),* Los Angeles County Museum of Art, 1967, No. 79 (ill.)
Lent by Dr. and Mrs. Albert S. Chase

Rico Lebrun was a humanist whose concerns as an artist were with the large themes of life: death, human suffering, religious faith, and redemption. The most basic influence on his work was seventeenth-century Baroque painting of his native Naples, whose dark view of life he shared even in sunny California. He spent several years as a fashionable

11 Rico Lebrun, *Genesis,* 1960, Frary Hall, Pomona College, Gift of Mr. and Mrs. Donald Winston

draftsman in New York, and then moved to California in 1938. There he produced his most penetrating visions, which were to culminate in the large Genesis mural of 1960 at Pomona College (fig. 11), which visitors to the exhibition in Claremont can study.

In the mid-1940s when he was artist-in-residence at the Santa Barbara Museum of Art, Lebrun spent a great deal of time in the ranchlands of the Santa Inez Valley. "Soon he became engrossed not only in the plant life that he observed, sketched and imbued with his own bristling spirit but also in the architecture, color and symbolic potential of farm machinery."[1]

[1]Henry J. Seldis, *Rico Lebrun,* Los Angeles County Museum of Art, 1966, p. 21.

WYNDHAM LEWIS
British, 1882–1957

40

Portrait of Olivia Shakespear, 1920 *(ill. p. 82)*
Pencil

Signed and dated in pen and ink, bottom left: "Wyndham
Lewis/1920"
16⁹/₁₆ x 10¾ in. (42 x 27.3 cm.)
Literature: Walter Michel, *Wyndham Lewis: Paintings and
Drawings,* London, 1971, No. 422; Santa Barbara Museum
of Art, *European Drawings in the Collection of the Santa Barbara
Museum of Art,* Alfred Moir ed., Santa Barbara, 1976,
pp. 144–5 (ill.)
Lent by the Santa Barbara Museum of Art, Gift of Wright
S. Ludington (41.2.17)

In 1914 Wyndham Lewis in the magazine *Blast* described
the ideals of the Vorticist movement of which he was the
leading spokesman. "By vorticism," he wrote, "we mean
(a) ACTIVITY as opposed to the tasteful PASSIVITY of
Picasso; (b) SIGNIFICANCE as opposed to the dull or
anecdotal character to which the Naturalist is condemned;
(c) ESSENTIAL MOVEMENT and ACTIVITY (such as the
energy of a mind) as opposed to the imitative cinematog-
raphy, the fuss and hysterics of the futurists."[1]

By 1920 the Vorticist movement, like Cubism and Futurism, was dead, but Lewis' drawings until the early 1920s
still reflected his desire for "ACTIVITY (such as the energy
of the mind)." Even without knowing the identity of the
sitter, one senses her complexity of character in the mixture
of hauteur in the stiff, erect neck; elegance in the sweeping
curves of the cape and the tiptoe positioning of her left foot;
and strength in the claw-like left hand and the dominance
of the face by the square jaw and small, beady eyes. Thus,
the energetic buildup of curves in the drawing is both
abstract and suggestive of personality.

The sitter was indeed a forceful character. She is Olivia
Shakespear, a minor novelist and the mother-in-law of Ezra
Pound. There is another portrait drawing of her also of 1920
in the collection of her grandson Omar Pound.[2]

[1]Quoted in Richard Buckle, *Jacob Epstein, Sculptor,* London,
1963, p. 65.
[2]Illustrated in Walter Michel, *Wyndham Lewis,* London,
1971, No. 484, Plate 46.

AUGUST MACKE
German, 1887–1914

41

Women at the Zoo, 1914 *(ill. p. 76)*
Pencil
10 x 8 in. (25.4 x 20.3 cm.)
Provenance: Peter Dietch Gallery, New York
Exhibitions: Fine Arts Gallery of San Diego, 1974; La Jolla
Museum of Contemporary Art, "The Kondon Collection,"
December 19, 1975–February 1, 1976.
Lent by Dr. Vance E. Kondon

12 August Macke, *Great Zoological Garden,* 1912, Museum an Ostwall
Dortmund, Collection Scäppel

Macke died in the first months of World War I. Early in his
career he had traveled widely with one of his patrons and
during a trip to Paris in 1907, he had been impressed by the
work of Cézanne. The major influence on his work, however,
was Cubism. Particularly in the work of Robert Delaunay
he found the desired combination of Cubist structure
and color. In 1914 he traveled to Algeria with Paul Klee
and Louis Moillet.

Macke and his close friend Franz Marc both enjoyed zoos. It
was there that Marc had studied animal anatomy, but what
particularly attracted Macke was the peculiar mixture of
nature and artifice to be found in zoos. He was above all a
painter of crowds, be they on the streets or in zoos. A comparison of this small drawing of early 1914 with a painting
of two years earlier (fig. 12) reveals a similar mixture of
animals and people within a decorative composition. In the
later work, however, the background has become more
abstract in its division into planes and textures. There con-
tinues to be a disparity between figures and landscape, a
separation which Macke overcomes only in the watercolors
of his Tunisian trip.

ARISTIDE MAILLOL
French, 1861–1944

42

Reclining Female Nude, c. 1920 (ill. p. 89)
Black chalk and gouache
Initialed within a circle, bottom right: "M"
10¹³/₁₆ x 7⁷/₁₆ in. (27.5 x 18.9 cm.)
Anonymous loan

Unlike the American sculptor Lachaise who also was preoccupied with the female nude, Aristide Maillol believed
that drawing was an essential ingredient in the process of
creating sculpture. We know that he retained many of his
studies after the model for decades, returning to them
frequently for ideas. According to Maillol it was, in fact,
possible to make a statue from a good drawing alone.[1]

13 Aristide Maillol, *Study for the Monument to Cézanne,* bronze, 1912, Paul Drey Gallery, New York

John Rewald has cogently described the types of Maillol's drawings:

> One can generally distinguish two different types among Maillol's drawings: those that were done from a model and that—independent from their greater or lesser "finish"—show his desire to stay close to the elements provided by nature; and those done from memory. These are almost always inspired by some decorative preoccupation: simplified lines are harmoniously assembled and convey a more general aspect in order to achieve compositions in which the body is, so to speak, a pretext for arabesques of great beauty.[2]

Nude Woman is one of Maillol's studies of a live model. It is characterized by a freshness of observation in its exploration of the figure's outlines—Maillol made frequent changes as he proceeded—and in the interior modeling. The media are charcoal and white gouache, which give a softness to the lines, reflecting Maillol's interest in volume.

A work of about 1920,[3] this drawing is connected with his many clay and bronze studies for the *Monument to Paul Cézanne,* the first of his major sculptures of a recumbent woman.

In both the illustrated study (fig. 13) and the drawing, the artist is fascinated by the protuberant abdomen and the twist of the upper torso. In the drawing he is also concerned with the distribution of weight created by the model's pose which results in a recumbent contra-posto, as it were, with a relaxed thrust out left hip, a weight-bearing right hip, and a lowered right shoulder.

[1]John Rewald, *Aristide Maillol: 1861–1944,* Solomon R. Guggenheim Museum, New York, 1975, p. 21.
[2]*Ibid.,* p. 21.
[3]Compare this drawing to catalogue numbers 123, 125, and 126, all drawings of 1920–1921, in Rewald's catalogue.

FRANZ MARC
German, 1880–1916

43

Colored Flowers, 1914 (ill. p. 74)
Mixed media
Pencil inscription on reverse: "Marc/Farbige Blumen"
8 x 6⁷⁄₁₆ in. (20.3 x 17.5 cm.)
Provenance: Estate of the artist; David B. Findlay, Inc., New York; Mr. and Mrs. Norton S. Walbridge, La Jolla
Exhibitions: Fine Arts Gallery of San Diego, "20th Century Tempo," June–August 1968; Fine Arts Gallery of San Diego, "20th Century Art," July–September 1970; Fine Arts Gallery of San Diego, "Color & Form: 1909–1914," No. 62, circulated to Oakland Museum of Art, Seattle Art Museum, 1972; Fine Arts Gallery of San Diego, summer 1974
Literature: Hermann Buneman, *Franz Marc—Zeichnungen und Aquarelle,* Munich, 1948, 1950, 1960 (color ill. p. 64); Bucheim, *Der Blaue Reiter,* 1959 (color ill. p. 171); Max Robinson, *Franz Marc Paintings,* New York, 1963, No. 12 (color ill.); *Realities,* May 1968 (color ill.); Klaus Lankheit, *Franz Marc, Catalog der Werke,* Cologne, 1970, No. 661 (ill); Henry G. Gardiner, *La Jolla Light,* December 16, 1971 (ill.); Fine Arts Gallery of San Diego, *Color & Form: 1909–1914,* 1972, No. 62 (color ill. p. 82)
Lent by the Fine Arts Gallery of San Diego, Gift of Mr. and Mrs. Norton S. Walbridge

Marc's art was a spiritual quest which led him, like the German Romanticists Runge and Friedrich before him, to try to express the secret life of nature. As early as 1908 he spoke of seeking "a pantheistic empathy with the vibration and flow of the blood of nature."[1]

Later he expressed his belief at more length:

> Art is metaphysical...it will free itself from man's purposes and desires. We will no longer paint the forest or the horse as they please us or appear to us, but as they really are, as the forest or the horse feel themselves—their absolute being—which lives behind the appearance which we see. We will be successful in so far as we can succeed in overcoming the traditional "logic" of millennia with artistic creativity. There are art forms which are abstract, which can never be proven by human knowledge. These forms have always existed, but were always obscured by human knowledge and desire. The faith in art itself was lacking, but we shall build it: it lives on the "other side."[2]

Colored Flowers shows Marc attempting to record the pulse of nature through the rhythms of flowers, leaves, trees, and mountain. Scale has been effectively distorted to emphasize the importance of simple flowers with their sweeping arch-like stems, so different in their inner being from the jagged mountain in the background. It is almost as if we are seeing nature as another flower might see it.

Marc had given up painting humans by the time the *Blaüe Reiter* group was formed with himself and Kandinsky as its leaders. By the end of 1914 he had abandoned even animals and plants and sought to reach the inner core of matter through pure abstraction.

Franz Marc, *Briefe, Aufzeichnungen und Aphorismen,* Berlin, 1920, Vol. I, p. 121.

[2]*Ibid.,* p. 121.

HENRI MATISSE
French, 1869–1954

44

Reclining Nude, c. 1922–1923 (ill. p. 87)
Pen and ink
Signed, bottom right: "Henri Matisse"
11 x 15½ in. (28 x 39.4 cm.)
Provenance: Estate of the artist; Gallerie Claude Bernard, Paris; Norton Simon, Inc., Museum of Art, Los Angeles
Exhibitions: John Berggruen Gallery, San Francisco, "Henri Matisse: An Exhibition of Selected Drawings in Homage to Frank Perls," September 18–October 25, 1975, circulated to Margo Leavin Gallery, Los Angeles, 1975, No. 9
Literature: Sotheby Parke Bernet, *Important 19th and 20th Century Paintings, Drawing and Sculpture,* Los Angeles, 1973, No. 33 (ill.); John Berggruen Gallery, *Henri Matisse,* San Francisco, 1975, No. 9 (ill.)
Lent by Mr. and Mrs. Eli Broad

In the early 1920s, Matisse made a large number of highly finished drawings of reclinging Odalisques, several of which were published in Eli Faure's *Henri Matisse* of 1923.[1]

Matisse in 1939 explained his interest in using the same model in many drawings:

> My models, human figures, are never just "dummies" in an interior. They are the principal theme in my work. I depend entirely on my model whom I observe at liberty, and then I decide on the pose which best suits her nature. When I take a new model, I guess the pose that will suit from the abandoned attitudes of repose, and then I become the slave of that pose. I often keep those girls several years, until interest is exhausted. My plastic signs probably express their souls (a word I dislike) which interests me subconsciously, or what else? Their forms are not always perfect, but they are always expressive. The emotional interest aroused in me by them does not necessarily appear particularly in the representation of their bodies, it is often, rather, in the lines by special values distributed over the whole canvas or paper, forming the orchestration or architecture. But not everyone sees this. It may be sublimated voluptuousness, and that may not be yet visible to everyone.[2]

[1]The one on page 53 is the same model in nearly the same pose as in this drawing. Two others are reproduced in Victor I. Carlson, *Matisse as a Draughtsman,* Baltimore Museum of Art, 1971, Nos. 37 and 38.
[2]Quoted in Raymond Escholier, *Matisse, A Portrait of the Artist and the Man,* New York, 1960, p. 124.

45

Head of a Woman, Number 1, 1937 (ill. p. 108)
Pen and ink
Signed and dated in pen and ink, bottom right: "Henri Matisse 37"
24¼ x 16⅛ in. (61.5 x 41 cm.)
Exhibitions: Frank Perls Gallery, Beverly Hills, 1952; Municipal Art Center, Long Beach, 1952; Art Galleries, University of California, Los Angeles, 1964; Art Galleries, University of California, Los Angeles, "Henri Matisse," circulated to Art Institute of Chicago and Boston Museum of Fine Arts, 1966; John Berggruen Gallery, San Francisco, "Henri Matisse: An Exhibition of Selected Drawings in Homage to Frank Perls," September 18–October 25, 1975, circulated to Margo Leavin Gallery, Los Angeles, 1975
Literature: "Evolution of a Painting, Henri Matisse: Blue Dress," *Magazine of Art* XXXII, No. 7, (1939), pp. 414–415; Alfred H. Barr, Jr., *Matisse, His Art and His Public,* New York, 1951, pp. 234–235, 251, 253; Art Galleries, University of California, Los Angeles, *From the Ludington Collection,* 1964, p. 29, No. 83; Jean Leymarie, Herbert Read, William C. Lieberman, *Henri Matisse,* Art Galleries, University of California, Los Angeles, 1966, pp. 155, 199, No. 184 (ill.); John Berggruen Gallery, San Francisco, *Henri Matisse,* 1975; Santa Barbara Museum of Art, *European Drawings in the Collection of the Santa Barbara Museum of Art,* Alfred Moir ed., Santa Barbara, 1976, pp. 66–67 (ill.)
Lent by the Santa Barbara Museum of Art, Gift of Wright S. Ludington (41.2.18)

Woman Number 1 is one of a series of highly finished drawings of Matisse's Russian model Lydia Delectorskaya.[1]

In 1939 Matisse explained his own drawings such as *Woman Number 1.* We quote at length because Matisse is so articulate:

> My line drawing is the purest and most direct translation of my emotion. Simplification of means allows that. But those drawings are more complete than they appear to some people who confuse them with a sketch. They generate light; looked at in a poor, or indirect light, they contain not only quality and sensibility, but also light and difference in values corresponding obviously to colour. Those qualities are also evident to many in full light. They derive from the fact that the drawings are always preceded by studies made in a less rigorous medium than line, charcoal or stump drawing, which enables one to consider simultaneously the character of the model, the human expression, the quality of surrounding light, atmosphere,

and all that can only be expressed in drawing. And it is not until I feel exhausted by that work, which may go on for several sessions, that I can with a clear mind give rein to my pen without hesitation. Then I feel clearly that my emotion is expressed in plastic writing. Once I have put my emotion into line and modelled the light of my white paper, without destroying its endearing whiteness, I can add or take away nothing further. The page is written: no correction is possible. If it is not sufficient, there is no other possibility than to begin again, as if it were an acrobatic feat....

I have always considered drawing not as an exercise of particular dexterity but as, above all, a means of expressing intimate feelings and moods, means simplified to give greater simplicity and spontaneity to expression, which should speak without heaviness directly to the mind of the spectator.[2]

[1]The relationship of this drawing to other drawings and paintings is fully examined in Patricia Cleek's entry in *European Drawings in the Collection of the Santa Barbara Museum of Art,* Alfred Moir ed., Santa Barbara, 1976, p. 66.
[2]From an interview in *Le Point,* quoted in Raymond Escholier, *Matisse, A Portrait of the Artist and the Man,* New York, 1960, pp. 123–124.

46

Still Life with Fruit, 1941 (ill. p. 109)
Pen and ink
Signed, bottom left: "Henri Matisse 41"
24½ x 19 in. (62.2 x 48.2 cm.)
Provenance: Leslie Waddington Galleries, London
Anonymous loan

While Matisse was always active as a draftsman, in 1941 and 1942 he was so inordinately productive that he even impressed himself. From Nice on April 3, 1942, he wrote his son: "For a year now I've been making an enormous effort in drawing. I say *effort* but that's a mistake, because what has occurred is a *floraison* after fifty years of effort..."[1] In 1943 many of these drawings were published in *Dessins: thèmes et variations.* Among them are two series of still-life drawings of 1941 (six in A and six in G). Those in A include the Chinese jar which plays so prominent a role in this drawing.

There are at least two other drawings similar in theme to this one (fig. 14).[2] All three include the artist drawing in the lower right corner. Matisse first included a fragment of himself in his drawings in about 1935. Earlier he had used mirrors to introduce the artist as part of his subject.

[1]Quoted in Alfred Barr, *Matisse: His Art and His Public,* Museum of Modern Art, New York, 1951, p. 268.
[2]A second is illustrated in Raymond Cogniat, *XX Century Drawings and Watercolors,* New York, 1972, p. 71.

14 Henri Matisse, *Still Life,* ink on paper, 1941, Leslie Waddington Gallery, London

MATTA (ROBERTO MATTA ECHAURREN)
Chilean, b. 1911

47

Untitled, c. 1940 (ill. p. 117)
Pencil, colored crayon, and collage
Inscribed, bottom: "Est-ce dons la vivre?...(sentence indecipherable), "La propieté sur la Jouissance"; Signed, bottom right: "Matta"
22⅜ x 28 in. (56.7 x 71.1 cm.) (sight)
Provenance: Richard Feigen Gallery, Chicago
Lent by Mrs. Nathan Alpers

Matta joined the Surrealist movement in 1937. Two years later he came to the United States where he was to remain for a decade before returning to Europe. He soon was at the center of the group which formed the nucleus of the so-called New York School.

In 1942 Matta (who had been an apprentice in Le Corbusier's Paris office in 1934) remarked, "Painting always has one foot in architecture, one foot in the dream."[1] In his draw-

ings of the early 1940s Matta explores both aspects—
architecture and dreams—in ways which do not appear in
his paintings until 1944.

The space in this drawing is not that of traditional one-
point perspective. Rather, there are several perspectives, and
the whole is a composite formed by the pasting together of
separate pieces of paper. It is a space—or spaces—that
needs to be organized and completed by the viewer. Matta,
in speaking of his strange perspective, said, "I want to
show the contradictions involved in reality. It is the space
created by contradictions, the space of *that* struggle, which
interests me as the best picture of our real condition. The
fault with most pictures today is that they show an *a priori*
freedom from which they have eliminated all contradiction,
all resemblance to reality."[2]

Inhabiting this tension-filled space are fantastic anthropo-
morphic beings participating in various forms of sexual
activity, a theme which pervades many of these early
1940s drawings.

[1]James Thrall Soby, "Matta Echaurren," *Magazine of Art,* XL
(1947), p. 104.
[2]William Rubin, *Matta,* Museum of Modern Art, New
York, 1957. p. 7.

JOAN MIRO
Spanish, b. 1893

48

La femme au collier (Woman with Necklace), 1937 *(ill. p. 110)*
Mixed media
Signed, bottom right: "Miro"
13 x 16 in. (33 x 40.6 cm.)
Provenance: Paul Kantor Gallery, Beverly Hills; Clifford
Odets; Pierre Matisse Gallery, New York
Exhibitions: Art Institute of Chicago, "20th International
Exhibition of Watercolors," 1941; Los Angeles County
Museum of Art, "Joan Miro Exhibition," June 10–July 21,
1959; Pasadena Art Museum, "Mr. and Mrs. Max Zurier
Collection," April 30–May 21, 1963, No. 44; Pasadena
Museum of Art, "Watercolors and Drawings from the
Zurier Collection," May, 1969; La Jolla Museum of Con-
temporary Art, "Paintings from the Collection of Mr. and
Mrs. Max Zurier," May 7–June 6, 1976
Lent by Mr. and Mrs. Max Zurier

In the twentieth century the most moving expression of the
horrors of war—with its slaughter and cruelty—has been
Picasso's *Guernica,* born of his reaction to the Spanish Civil
War. Picasso's fellow Spaniard Joan Miro was also deeply
disturbed by this war which presaged the horrors of World

ERRATA
The correct information on *MIRO,* Cat. No. 48 is:
Group of Personages, 1937
Pen, ink and watercolor
Signed, lower right: "Miro"; signed and dated on verso:
"Miro 30/9/37"
18⅞ x 24¾ in. (48 x 63 cm.)
Provenance: Paul Kantor Gallery, Beverly Hills
Exhibitions: Pasadena Art Museum, "Mr. and Mrs. Max
Zurier Collection," April 30–May 21, 1963, No. 43;
Pasadena Museum of Art, "Watercolors and Drawings from
the Zurier Collection," May, 1969; La Jolla Museum of
Contemporary Art, "Paintings from the Collection of Mr.
and Mrs. Max Zurier," May 7–June 6, 1976
Literature: Jacques Dupin, *Joan Miro,* New York, 1962,
Plate 58, p. 276
Lent by Mr. and Mrs. Max Zurier

The measurements for Plate 58 in Jacques Dupin's *Joan
Miro* are incorrect, being the result of a typographical error.
This signed and dated (September 30, 1937) watercolor is
the one reproduced in Dupin, Plate 58.

AMADEO MODIGLIANI
Italian, 1884–1920

49

Portrait of François Bernouard, 1917–1918 (ill. p. 82)
Pencil
Inscribed, left side: "Mon cher ami Bernouard/Modigliani"
18¼ x 11¼ in. (46.3 x 28.6 cm.)
Provenance: Felix Landau Gallery, Los Angeles
Exhibitions: Musée National d'Art Moderne, Paris, "Le
Dessin de Toulouse-Lautrec aux Cubistes," June–October
1954, No. 156; Musée Cantini, Marseilles, "Modigliani,"
June 10–July 27, 1958, No. 62; Palazzo Reale, Milan,
"Mostra di Amadeo Modigliani," November–December
1958, No. 146; Galleria Nazionale d'Art Moderna, Rome,
"Modigliani," January–February 1959, No. 103; Felix
Landau Gallery, Los Angeles, "Modern Masters Drawings and
Watercolors," April 3–29, 1967, No. 31; Fine Arts Gallery
of San Diego, "20th Century Tempo," July–September
1968; Fine Arts Gallery of San Diego, "20th Century Art,"
July–September 1970
Literature: Jeanne Modigliani, *Modigliani: Man and Myth,*
New York, 1958 (Pl. 94); Lamberto Vitali, *Quarantacinque
desegni di Modigliani,* Turin, 1959 (Pl. 33a); Felix Landau
Gallery, *Modern Masters Drawings and Watercolors,* Los
Angeles, 1967, No. 31 (ill.)
Anonymous loan

Modigliani's friend Francois Bernouard (1884–1949) was thirty-three or thirty-four at the time of this portrait. Bernouard was an editor who published excellent editions of the complete works of Zola, Jules Renard, Elemir Bourges, Gerard de Nerval, and others. He also published deluxe editions of poetry anthologies.

Modigliani captures the sensitivity of his friend by means of the typically long neck, the tilt of the head, and the economical rendering of the face. As in his painted portraits, Modigliani concentrates upon the most salient and psychologically revealing features: only one eye and half of the nose are fully delineated and shaded.

HENRY MOORE
English, b. 1898

50

Heads (No. 2) (Interior and Exterior Forms), 1950 *(ill. p. 130)*
Colored crayons, watercolor, and wash
Signed and dated, bottom right: "Moore 50"; Titled on verso
15½ x 22½ in. (39.4 x 57.2 cm.)
Provenance: Curt Valentin, New York; M. Knoedler and Co., Inc., New York; Richard Feigen Gallery, Chicago; B. C. Holland Gallery, Chicago; Mr. and Mrs. Lester Francis Avnet, New York; Piccadilly Gallery, London; Sale, Sotheby Parke Bernet, Inc., March 18, 1976, No. 87
Exhibitions: The Arts Club of Chicago, "Henry Moore Sculpture and Drawings from Chicago Collections," 1960, No. 77; Richard Feigen Gallery, Chicago, "Important Recent Acquisitions," 1960, No. 22; New York Cultural Center, "A Selection of Drawings, Pastels, and Watercolors from the Collection of Mr. and Mrs. Lester Francis Avnet," 1969–1970, No. 93
Literature: Richard Feigen Gallery, *Important Recent Acquisitions,* Chicago, 1960, No. 22 (ill.); New York Cultural Center, *A Selection of Drawings, Pastels, and Watercolors from the Collection of Mr. and Mrs. Lester Francis Avnet,* New York, 1969–1970, No. 93 (ill.); Sotheby Parke Bernet, Inc., *Important 19th and 20th Century Drawings and Watercolors Collected by the Late Lester Avnet,* March 18, 1976, No. 87 (color ill.)
Lent by Mr. and Mrs. Eli Broad

Moore first discovered the helmet form in 1939. In a series of drawings and sculpture he found in the form, "the cranial equivalent of the internal-external forms; heads which should have the same degree of metamorphosis, the same intensity as the bodies of his reclining figures."[1]

In 1950 he returned to the helmet heads in both sculpture and drawings. Erich Neumann in *The Archetypal World of Henry Moore* posits an interesting interpretation of *Helmet No. 2* (fig. 15) and the whole series. He says—and I quote at length:

15 Henry Moore, *Helmet Head No. 2,* bronze, 1950, Collection of Dorothy and Richard Sherwood, Los Angeles

The polarity and unity of this structure come from the balanced contrast between the outer form as the container and the inner form contained within it. As in the 1940 helmet, the head is like a maternal uterus with an embryonic creature inside. An interior being, having by nature a curious independence, as we shall see, gazes outward through the windows of the body casing. What we spoke of earlier as the archetypal constellation of soul dwelling "in" the body is here concretized in a new way, and the common human experience that in a person's face there is an inner being looking out through the eyes of the body has become plastic reality. . . .

These inner beings, if one surveys Moore's development as a whole, prove to be little totalities, complete soul figures. This is obvious enough when we remember that for many years the head often had a double form in his sculptures. The bipolar top of the interior figure, which stares out here like a pair of eyes from inside the helmet, has long been for Moore a typical symbol for the whole head. This means that the little figures peering out of the head like souls are really little "men" or "persons," an archaic idea that is still preserved in speech, for the "pupil" of the eye (*pupilla, pupula*) originally meant a baby girl or doll. The living but invisible dweller within is made visible as the interior life of the shell, its animating principle. What gives this head its frightening and spectral appearance, however, is not its novel form but the stark, staring terror of the soul as it looks out of its rigid encasement. This terrified and terrifying expression is heightened by the motif of "imprisonment," which we met earlier in another form. The figure in the helmet seems to be gazing not so much out of a window as out of the window of a prison.[2]

The fierceness and imprisoning sense of the sculpture is somewhat mitigated in the drawing by the warmth of the gray and maroon colors. Moore started using color in his drawings in the 1940s to enhance the drama and to create atmosphere. As is typical of many of his drawings, he fills the entire page, creating a highly finished work of art. Also typical is his tiering of the helmets into two rows, a compositional device he began using in the 1930s and was to use frequently in the lithographs of the 1950s.

[1]Kenneth Clark, *Henry Moore Drawings,* London, 1974, p. 222.
[2]Erich Neumann, *The Archetypal World of Henry Moore,* New York, 1959, pp. 103–105.

GIORGIO MORANDI
Italian, 1890–1964

51

Still Life of Bottles, 1957 (ill. p. 130)
Pencil
Signed and dated in pencil, bottom center: "Morandi/1957"
6½ x 9⅜ in. (16.5 x 23.8 cm.)
Provenance: New World Gallery, New York
Literature: Santa Barbara Museum of Art, *European Drawings in the Collection of the Santa Barbara Museum of Art,* Alfred Moir ed., Santa Barbara, 1976, pp. 210–211 (ill.)
Lent by the Santa Barbara Museum of Art, Gift of Mrs. MacKinley Helm (69.35.32)

Giorgio Morandi has often been called the twentieth-century Chardin because of his highly refined still-life paintings. His career began in the teens of this century when he was briefly influenced by Giorgio de Chirico's metaphysical paintings. His concern with the subtle connections among things—usually bottles, jars, and boxes—dates from the beginning of his career. In this late drawing of 1957, he emphasized the two-dimensionality of objects by creating a single base line for the items stacked behind each other in space: the bottle and pitcher, two favorite motifs of that year, as well as the indications of a bottle at the left and a box at the right. The asymmetrical placement of the composition upon the page creates an added interest in this apparently simple, but actually complex drawing.

ROBERT MOTHERWELL
American, b. 1915

52

Displaced Table, 1943 (ill. p. 121)
Collage
Signed and dated, bottom right: "R. Motherwell 43"
40 x 30 in. (101.6 x 76.2 cm.)
Provenance: Art of this Century, New York; Dwight Ripley, New York; Robert Elkon Gallery, New York
Exhibitions: San Francisco Museum of Art, "Abstract and Surrealist Art in the United States," 1944, No. 63
Lent by Mr. Robert H. Halff and Mr. Carl W. Johnson

Robert Motherwell spent the year 1938 in Paris following graduate work at Harvard. His collages of the early 1940s show the influence of the "French" tradition of Picasso, Matisse, and Mondrian with its restrained, classical elegance which Motherwell has always admired. His collage technique derives from Cubism, and like those of Kurt Schwitters (see Cat. No. 67), Motherwell's collages demonstrate the triumph of taste and sensibility over material.

At the same time Motherwell was interested in the automatism of the Surrealists. These early collages show an interest "as well in the freely painted areas and lines, created automatically or by doodling, with semi-illusionistic atmosphere surrounding the flat areas."[1]

The title *Displaced Table* refers to the position of the table top which is seen directly from above and has fruit drawn upon it. A door, also viewed from above, is at the upper right. This "interior" is controlled by a strong central vertical "spine," a compositional device Motherwell learned from Picasso.

Motherwell believes in the associational meanings of abstract art. These meanings, however, do not have precise verbal equivalents but rather deal with "... felt experience—intense, immoderate, direct, subtle, unified, warm, vivid, rhythmic."[2]

[1]E. A. Carmean, Jr., *The Collages of Robert Motherwell,* Museum of Fine Arts, Houston, 1972, p. 11.
[2]Quoted in Edward B. Henning, "Some Contemporary Paintings," *Bulletin of the Cleveland Museum,* 49 (March, 1962), p. 51.

53

Spanish Elegy (Molina de Segura), 1953 (ill. p. 126)
Brush and ink
Initialed, bottom right: "R.M."
11¾ x 14½ in. (29.8 x 36.8 cm.)
Provenance: Kootz Gallery, New York; Primus Gallery, Los Angeles; Margo Leavin Gallery, Los Angeles

Exhibitions: Otis Art Institute Gallery, Motherwell retrospective, November 1974, No. 13
Literature: Otis Art Institute Gallery, *Robert Motherwell in California Collections,* Los Angeles, 1974, No. 13 (ill.)
Lent by Jackie and Manny Silverman

Motherwell began his series of *Elegies to the Spanish Republic* in 1948. It is a series concerned exclusively with death, a theme which haunted Motherwell as a child. The first foreign political event which engaged his feelings was the Spanish Civil War. Frank O'Hara has described the power of the series:

> The Spanish Elegies vary radically in size and even at their smallest are no longer easel paintings, but arenas in which the ceremony takes place "at five in the afternoon." Here the scale is determined in inverse ratio to emotional empathy; in the large elegies one is caught in the inexorable and cruel formality of the action close up; in the small elegies one is at a distance, contemplating the pathos of the event. Almost liturgical in their progression, the elegies are the first American paintings to use black and white in a full symbolic sense: the white of purity, of light, of experience, which cuts into the dominating black forms of death briefly and is ultimately conquered, may be reversed in meaning because of the ritual sense of the event. The blacks are more vibrant, more living, in these paintings than the whites or earthy ochres, perhaps signifying that death with honor is indeed life-in-death.[1]

[1]Frank O'Hara, *Robert Motherwell,* Pasadena Art Museum, 1962, not paginated.

ELIE NADELMAN
Polish/American, 1882–1946

54

Three Birds, c. 1920 (ill. p. 92)
Brush, black, brown, and blue ink
6⅞ x 6⅞ in. (17.5 x 17.5 cm.)
Provenance: E. Weyhe Gallery, New York
Lent by Mr. Vincent Price

Elie Nadelman, the Polish-born sculptor who came to America as a young man, made several drawings of hens and cocks.[1] They are close in style and date to the *Three Birds.* All share the same closed contours, elegant, simplified shapes, and volume implied through the use of washes, exemplified here by the blue-black sweep of male breast to the tip of the tail. The peacock is shown after the shedding of his fancy tail feathers, and the peahens are, as always, rather drab.

The poultry drawings were partly inspired by Pennsylvania-German drawings. Nadelman had many such drawings in his collection of family blessings, birth and death certificates, and magical Hex symbols.

Although Nadelman produced several ducks in polished marble, none of these poultry drawings seem to be related to specific sculptures.

[1]Lincoln Kirstein, *Elie Nadelman Drawings,* New York, 1949, No. 58.

EMIL NOLDE
German, 1867–1956

55

Red and Gold Sunflowers (ill. p. 103)
Watercolor
Signed, center bottom: "Nolde"
18¼ x 13 in. (46.3 x 33 cm.)
Provenance: Marlborough Gallery, London
Exhibitions: Pasadena Museum of Modern Art, "German Expressionist Painting and Sculpture from California Collections," April 16–June 2, 1974
Lent by Mr. and Mrs. Philip S. Brown

Flowers were one of Nolde's favorite subjects in both his oil paintings and watercolors. Some of his finest early paintings are of gardens, and he maintained a garden wherever he was, even on the North German coast where flower gardens were unknown. At Seebull, the house which he built, he arranged the flower beds to form the initials "A" and "E" for Ada and Emil. As Peter Selz has cogently remarked, "Nolde's taste was a peculiar combination of middle-class banality and unique individuality."[1]

Nolde paints his flowers as close-ups, showing no interest in the complete plant. Yet he saw flowers as symbols of the cycle of life. In his autobiography he wrote: "The blossoming colors of the flowers and the purity of those colors—I love them. I loved the flowers and their fate: shooting up, blooming, radiating, glowing, gladdening, bending, wilting, thrown away and dying."[2]

[1]Peter Selz, *Emil Nolde,* Museum of Modern Art, New York, 1963, p. 49.
[2]Emil Nolde, *Jahre der Kampfe,* Berlin, 1934, p. 93.

56

North German Landscape (ill. p. 102)
Watercolor
Signed, bottom right: "Nolde"
14¼ x 17⅛ in. (35.8 x 43.4 cm.)
Provenance: Anne Abels Gallery, Cologne
Exhibitions: La Jolla Museum of Contemporary Art, "The Kondon Collection," December 19, 1975–February 1, 1976
Lent by Dr. Vance E. Kondon

16 Ada and Emil Nolde in 1902

Emil Nolde's family lived on the same farm on the North German coast for nine generations. His attachment to this wild and rugged landscape is evident in his having taken as his last name the name of the town closest to the farm, Nolde. The name change occurred in 1900 when he gave up his natal Hansen to symbolize his rebirth as an artist.

The landscape of the region, with its open marshlands and nearby North Sea, played a prominent role in Nolde's work, and it was there that he returned to live permanently. In this work the glowing effect of the lingering summer twilight dominates the flat, desolate landscape.

57

Lovers, (Portrait of the Artist and His Wife), 1932 (ill. p. 104)
Watercolor
Signed, bottom right: "Nolde"
13½ x 19 in. (34.2 x 48.2 cm.)
Provenance: Schweide Collection, Berlin; Ala Story, Santa Barbara
Exhibitions: Pomona College, "German Expressionist Painting, 1910–1950," October 25–November 23, 1957, No. 38; Phoenix Art Museum, "Paintings, Drawings and Sculpture from the Collection of Margaret Mallory and Ala Story," 1962; Museum of Modern Art, New York, "Emil Nolde," circulated to San Francisco Museum of Modern Art, and Pasadena Art Museum, 1963 No. 94; Santa Barbara Museum of Art, "Two Collections," January 15–February 20, 1966, No. 46, circulated to California Palace of the Legion of Honor, 1966; Colorado Springs Fine Arts Center, 1971; The Art Institute of Chicago, 1972
Literature: Peter Selz, *Emil Nolde,* Museum of Modern Art, New York, 1963, No. 94, p. 69; Santa Barbara Museum of Art, *Two Collections,* 1966, No. 46 (ill.)
Lent by Margaret Mallory

We know more about the origins of Nolde's *Lovers, (Self Portrait of the Artist and His Wife)* than of most of Nolde's watercolors. Professor Iso Brante Schweide, to whom Nolde gave the watercolor as a parting present, wrote in a letter of July 15, 1957, to Ala Story:

> The watercolor of the very dramatically conceived figures of early 1932 was created during one night when Nolde suddenly jumped out of bed and in his dressing gown ran into his atelier to get freed of the vision of figures in which he symbolized the love of his very own happiness. His wife Ada was amazed by the sudden awakening of Emil, and she told me in his presence that when the composition of the two figures was finished, he took a deep breath and said to her, "This is our best portrait of our superior being." And then, she said, "Emil worked as though obsessed and he refused to sit down and have breakfast as he could not leave the picture until it was finished."

The story is revealing of many traits in Nolde's art. The feverish haste in which the *Lovers* was created was typical of his approach; in his early garden paintings, those paintings which attracted the *Brücke* artists to the older Nolde, he had squeezed the colors directly from the tube unto the canvas in a frenzy of activity. It was his belief that a work of art should be created in one sitting, while the red-hot inspiration lasted, that led Nolde to concentrate on watercolor. And, he became one of the leading twentieth-century masters in this medium.

The story is revealing as well of Nolde's visionary fantasies. In the early 1930s he did a series of watercolors in which, for example, he painted fantastic couples such as a monkey and a witch. Strange couples—old men with beautiful young girls, dark men and lovely blondes—had fascinated Nolde (and many other German artists) for years. In the *Lovers* the contrast between the dark, brooding artist and the demure blonde Ada is psychologically haunting. An intense, but inward battle of the sexes is being portrayed between young lovers. A desire for an inner truth led Nolde to distort physical reality: the lovers are young, while Nolde was actually 65 at the time of this work; his nose in reality had a decided hook to it, and even in 1902, when he and Ada married, he had had very little hair (fig. 16).

Nolde said of the watercolor: "This is our best portrait of our superior beings." The *Lovers* can thus be interpreted as a portrayal of the ardent artist caught in a moment of visionary intensity. His beautiful wife, standing beside him, while not partaking in the fervor of the moment, harmonizes with him in her calmness.

The style of the watercolor with its scratchy, thin pen strokes and broad washes of color anticipates the "Unpainted Pictures" produced later in the 1930s, while the quality of the lines is reminiscent of the etchings of the teens.

MAX PECHSTEIN
German, 1881–1955

58

Resting Woman with Mirror, 1910 (ill. p. 72)
Brush and ink
Signed and dated on verso, top right: "Pechstein 1910"
20¾ x 17 in. (52.7 x 43.2 cm.)
Provenance: Hannah Beliker von Roth, Frankfurterkunst Kabinett, Frankfurt
Exhibitions: La Jolla Museum of Contemporary Art, "The Kondon Collection," December 19, 1975–February 1, 1976
Lent by Dr. Vance E. Kondon

Max Pechstein was a member of the *Brücke* both in Dresden and Berlin. He once described artistic creation as analogous to childbearing: "When you draw seek God within you; do not say 'I will' but 'So be it'... the work arises! No task! Painful and joyful is the exultation of giving birth."[1] Usually more superficial than the others in the *Brücke*, Pechstein could occasionally be very forceful as a draftsman, as in this drawing of 1910. The bold, rough lines, most economical in their modeling, are similar in power to those in his lithographs of this period.

[1]Quoted in Peter Selz, *German Expressionist Painting*, Berkeley, 1957, p. 111.

PABLO PICASSO
Spanish, 1881–1973

59

Italian Peasants, 1919 (ill. p. 85)
Pencil and smeared charcoal
Signed and dated in pencil, bottom left: "Picasso/19"
35¼ x 29¾ in. (89.5 x 75.5 cm.)
Provenance: Gallerie de l'Effort Moderne, Paris
Exhibitions: The Denver Art Museum, "Ten by Ten," February–June, 1954; McKay Art Institute, San Antonio, "Inaugural Exhibition," 1954, No. 23; Contemporary Arts Association, Houston, "Picasso," January 14–February 20, 1955, No. 16; Museum of Modern Art, New York, "Picasso: Seventy-Fifth Anniversary Exhibition," 1957; The Art Institute of Chicago, October 29–December 8, 1957; Philadel-

phia Museum of Art, 1958, No. 86; La Jolla Museum of Art, 1960; Cheney Cowles Museum of Eastern Washington State Historical Society, Spokane, 1961; University of California, Los Angeles, "Bonne Fête Monsieur Picasso," 1961, No. 77; The Art Gallery of Toronto and Montreal Museum of Fine Arts, "Picasso and Man," 1964; Chicago, February 28–March 11, 1966; The Portland (Oregon) Art Association, "Picasso for Portland," September 21–October 25, 1970
Literature: Christian Zervos, *Pablo Picasso*, Paris, 1949, Vol. III, No. 431; McKay Art Institute, *Inaugural Exhibition*, San Antonio, 1954, No. 23; Contemporary Arts Association, *Picasso*, Houston, 1955, No. 16; Alfred H. Barr Jr., ed., *Picasso: Seventy-Five Anniversary Exhibition*, Museum of Modern Art, New York, 1957, p. 49 (ill.); M. Maurice Jardot, *Drawings of Pablo Picasso*, New York, 1959, No. 49 p. 155; University of California, Los Angeles, *Bonne Fête Monsieur Picasso*, Los Angeles, 1961, No. 77; Jean S. Boggs, *Picasso and Man*, The Art Gallery of Toronto, 1964, No. 71; The Arts Club of Chicago, *Fiftieth Anniversary of the Arts Club*, Chicago, 1966, No. 91; Santa Barbara Museum of Art, *European Drawings in the Collection of the Santa Barbara Museum of Art*, Alfred Moir ed., Santa Barbara, 1976, p. 259 (ill.)
Lent by Santa Barbara Museum of Art, Gift of Wright S. Ludington (46.10.2)

By 1919 Cubism had ceased to interest Picasso. In his new appreciation for realism, he looked to different sources—one of which was photography. According to Maurice Jardot,[1] *Italian Peasants* was drawn after a postcard which Picasso had picked up on a trip to Italy. At this time, Picasso was also becoming interested in ballet design, and Jean Boggs has suggested that he found "the contrast between the uniform and the peasant costume a picturesque one."[2] The illusionism of the source is counteracted by Picasso's emphasis on the hard clarity of the outlines and in his very sparing use of modeling. He used the draftsman's technique of cross-hatching in the shading of the costumes, the necks, and the faces of the two figures.

[1]M. Maurice Jardot, *Drawings of Pablo Picasso*, New York, 1959, No. 49, p. 155.
[2]Jean Sutherland Boggs, *Picasso and Man*, Art Gallery of Toronto, 1964, p. 82.

60

Woman Before a Mirror, 1934 (ill. p. 107)
Pen and ink, gouache, colored chalks, and pastel
Signed, bottom right: "Picasso"; Dated, center top: "Paris 11 Avril XXXIV"
9⅜ x 13¾ in. (23.8 x 34.9 cm.)
Provenance: Mr. and Mrs. William Preston Harrison
Literature: Los Angeles County Museum of Art, *Drawings in the Collection of the Los Angeles County Museum of Art*, 1970 (ill., n.p.)

17 Pablo Picasso, *Girl Before a Mirror,* 1932, Museum of Modern Art, New
York, Gift of Mrs. Simon Guggenheim

Lent by the Los Angeles County Museum of Art, the
Mr. and Mrs. William Preston Harrison Collection

One of Picasso's most famous paintings of the early 1930s is
Girl Before a Mirror of 1932 in the Museum of Modern Art
(fig. 17) in which he explored the complexity of a figure and
its reflection. He had treated the same theme ten years
earlier in a dry point which, however, has none of the complexity of the later painting.[1] The drawing of 1934 is closer
to the earlier work in its concentration on the simple act
of a woman examining herself.

In April of 1934 Picasso had finished just a few months
earlier the illustrations for Aristophanes' *Lysistrata.* Those
scenes of dalliance are characterized by the variety of patterns and linear rhythms. In *Woman Before a Mirror* Picasso
adapted his style to the subject. It is a night scene lit only
by a candle before the mirror. In the darkness of the heavily
curtained room, the nude woman is lost in lustful abandon.
Her back is arched, her arms behind her tilted head. A
bearded head peers through the window at the right. The
work is marked by the variety of media employed and by
the linear variations—from the heavy lines and repeated
crosshatchings of the mirror to the delicate swirling embel-
lishments of the body.

[1]Illustrated in Bernhard Geiser, *Picasso, Peintre-Graveur,*
Vol. II, Bern, 1968, No. 69.

JACKSON POLLOCK
American, 1912–1956

61

Number 4, 1948 (ill. p. 123)
Enamel on gesso on paper
Signed and dated, bottom right (signed and titled in 1949):
"Jackson Pollock 49"
22⅝ x 30⅞ in. (57.4 x 78.4 cm.)
Provenance: Betty Parsons Gallery, New York; Museum of
Modern Art, New York; Betty Parsons Gallery; Frank
Kinnicut; Betty Parsons Gallery
Exhibition: Betty Parsons Gallery (works from 1948),
January–February 1949; Museum of Modern Art, New
York, "Jackson Pollock: Works on Paper," circulated to
Walker Art Center, University of Maryland, Museum of
Contemporary Art, Chicago, Seattle Art Museum, Baltimore
Art Museum, Montreal Museum of Fine Arts, Rose Art
Museum, Brandeis University, 1968–1969
Literature: Bernice Rose, *Jackson Pollock: Works on Paper,*
Museum of Modern Art, New York, 1969, p. 64 (ill.)
Lent by the Weisman Collection of Art

In the winter of 1946–1947 Jackson Pollock began to develop his "drip" paintings in which he dripped and poured
enamel paint directly onto a horizontal surface. By 1948
he had adapted this technique to works on paper as well,
producing in both media a final solution which is radically
graphic in execution. Pollock was a master in his control of
line—particularly with a stick. He was able: "to quicken
a line by thinning it, to slow it by flooding, to elaborate that
simplest of elements, the line—to change, to reinvigorate,
to extend, to build up an embarrassment of riches in the
mass by drawing alone. And each change in the individual
line is what every draftsman has always dreamed of: color."[1]

In a series of drawings of 1948 we can trace the development
of Pollock's mature "drip" style. This drawing is dated
1949, but it was actually one of those executed early in
1948.[2] In it we can see how Pollock forced figures: "to extend themselves into abstract lines." This underlying figurative drawing becomes, in the later works of 1948, the "underground" over which structural lines are "hung," to build
up the composition in "invisible planes."

Pollock contended that his work was not non-objective,
saying he "veiled" the images. Bernice Rose has explained
this apparent paradox:

> What is at stake in this kind of seeming paradox is a
> conscious surrealist/Jungian conception of the work as a
> metaphor for an evocative but deliberately controlled
> chaos, in which accident, except in the Freudian sense,
> is denied. Specific figures are subsumed or transcended
> as the work approaches "the deeper layer of the psyche"

and becomes a representation of the unconscious—a parallel to the chaos at the heart of the matter."[3]

[1]Frank O'Hara, *Jackson Pollock*, New York, 1959, p. 26.
[2]Bernice Rose, *Jackson Pollock: Works on Paper*, Museum of Modern Art, New York, 1969, p. 64.
[3]*Ibid.*, p. 16.

MAURICE PRENDERGAST
American, 1859–1924

62

Picnic, c. 1915 (ill. p. 90)
Watercolor
Signed, bottom left: "Prendergast"
13½ x 18¼ in. (34.3 x 46.3 cm.)
Provenance: Dalzell Hatfield Galleries, Los Angeles
Exhibitions: State College Art Department, San Diego, April 1964; University of New Mexico, Albuquerque, "Impressionism in America," February–March 1965, No. 43, circulated to M. H. de Young Memorial Museum; Los Angeles County Museum of Art, "Eight American Masters of Watercolor," April–June 1968, No. 41, circulated to M. H. de Young Memorial Museum, Seattle Art Museum, 1968; Phoenix Art Museum, "The Eight," April–May 1977
Literature: Fine Arts Gallery of San Diego, *Catalogue*, 1960, XXX, p. 7; Fine Arts Gallery of San Diego, *Master Works from the Collection of the Fine Arts Gallery of San Diego*, 1968 (ill.); Larry Curry, *Eight American Masters of Watercolor*, Los Angeles, 1968, No. 41; O. Dekom, *Evening Journal*, Delaware, January 20, 1969 (ill.)
Lent by the Fine Arts Gallery of San Diego

Maurice Prendergast was the oldest member of the group of American artists known as the Eight. He visited Europe in the early 1890s, and upon his return to America slowly freed himself from a detailed, rather academic (although brilliantly executed) watercolor style. In 1907, the year of the Fauve exhibition and the Cézanne retrospective—he returned to France and excitedly observed the new style. The following year he participated in the exhibition of the Eight.

The very fresh watercolor *Picnic* is a late work by Prendergast. The subject—a group of women arranged frieze-like in a landscape—is a typical one for the artist. So, too, are the loose brushstrokes which rapidly sketch in the faceless group to form a harmonious, decorative design.

GEORGES ROUAULT
French, 1871–1958

63

Ballerina and Two Clowns, c. 1930 (ill. p. 106)
Gouache
Signed, bottom center: "G. Rouault"
16 x 11¼ in. (40.6 x 28.5 cm.)
Provenance: Leslie Waddington Galleries, London
Anonymous loan

Georges Rouault studied under the Symbolist painter Gustave Moreau, who appreciated and nurtured his talent. His paintings of the early years of the century concentrated on serious subjects: the sad life of prostitutes and religious themes. In 1902 he painted his first work devoted to the circus, and he soon developed this theme in a number of paintings of clowns and ballerinas. He explained his fascination for circus characters:

> ...for myself, ever since the end of one lovely day when the first star to shine in the sky clutched at my heart, I can't say why, unconsciously, I have derived from this instant an entire system of poetics. That gypsy wagon standing on the side of the road, the emaciated old horse grazing on the thin grass, the aging clown sitting beside his wagon mending his bright, multicolored costume—the contrast between brilliant, scintillating things intended to amuse us, and this infinitely sad life, if one looks at it a bit objectively...Then, I expanded it all. I saw clearly that the "clown" was myself, ourselves...almost all of us...that this rich, spangled costume is given us by life, we're all of us clowns, more or less, we all wear a "spangled costume," but if we are caught unawares, the way I caught that old clown, tell me![1]

In the early 1930s Rouault made eighty-two gouaches of circus themes. These were reproduced in wood engravings and together with seventeen colored etchings were part of the book *Cirque de l'Etoile Filante*, published by Vollard in 1938. It is possible that this gouache is one of the eighty-two used for this book.[2] The gouache has also been dated 1917–1918.

The pose struck by the ballerina—arms crossed and leg relaxed—appears in many of Rouault's works of the late 1920s and early 1930s. In the gouache he altered the figure—she is now considerably thinner in the hips—to emphasize the rhythmical sway of the leg. His use of heavy lines gives the figure a definite sense of solidity and also of isolation which is heightened by the somber background.

[1]Quoted in Pierre Courthion, *Georges Rouault*, New York, 1961, p. 86.
[2]I have been unable to study a copy of the book, but this gouache is the same size as another produced for the book; it is illustrated in Courthion, p. 287.

EGON SCHIELE
Austrian, 1890–1918

64

The Embrace, 1915 (ill. p. 75)
Tempera and charcoal
Signed and dated, bottom right: "Egon Schiele 1915"
12 x 16½ in. (30.5 x 41.9 cm.)
Provenance: Gallerie St. Etienne, Paris; Ala Story
Collection, Santa Barbara
Exhibitions: Phoenix Art Museum, "Paintings, Sculpture
and Drawings from the Collection of Margaret Mallory
and Ala Story," 1962; University of California, Berkeley,
"Viennese Expressionism 1910–1924," 1963 No. 67, cir-
culated to Pasadena Art Museum, 1963; Santa Barbara
Museum of Art, "Two Collections," January 15–February
20, 1966, No. 48, circulated to California Palace of the
Legion of Honor, 1966
Literature: Herschel B. Chipp, *Viennese Expressionism 1910–
1924,* University of California, Berkeley, 1963, No. 67 (ill.);
Santa Barbara Museum of Art, *Two Collections,* 1966, No. 48
Lent by Margaret Mallory

It is hard to realize that Schiele died when he was only
twenty-eight. In his short lifetime he attacked Viennese
façades, both artistic and moral. He selected as his special
goal "the exposure of his society's hypocritical and repressive
attitude towards sex."[1] In paintings and drawings he
treated such taboo subjects as copulation, masturbation, and
Lesbian love. This audacity and his openness about his life
with his mistress Walli led Schiele to be charged in a trial
of 1912 with "immorality" and "seduction," an event which
led to twenty-four days imprisonment and which further
clouded his already tempestuous life.

In 1915 he foresook Walli to marry Edith Harms. As a grue-
some parting tribute to his mistress, he painted one of his
most haunting paintings, the allegorical self-portrait *Death
and the Maiden.* In that same year he produced *The Embrace.*
The drawing is marked by an unusual viewpoint: we
see the couple from above; their swirling forms seem to be
floating in space as if they were celestial lovers creating their
own galaxy.

The drawing is related to two others of 1915 in which
Schiele depicted the same two women in poses of more
earthy passion: *Two Girls Lying Entwined* in the Albertina
and *Two Girls Embracing Each Other* in the Museum of Fine
Arts, Budapest.[2]

[1] Allessandra Comini, *Egon Schiele,* New York, 1976, p. 10.
[2] Illustrated in Erwin Mitsch, *The Art of Egon Schiele,* New
York, 1975, Fig. 55 and Pl. 56.

Two Standing Nudes, 1918 (ill. p. 77)
Black crayon
Signed and dated, bottom right: "Egon Schiele 1918"
18¼ x 11⅝ in. (46.3 x 29.5 cm.)
Provenance: Eric Estorick, London; Grosvenor
Gallery, London
Exhibitions: University of California, Berkeley, "Viennese
Expressionism 1910–1924," February 5–March 10, 1963,
No. 85, circulated to the Pasadena Art Museum, 1963.
Literature: Herschel B. Chipp, *Viennese Expressionism 1910–
1924,* University of California, Berkeley, 1963, No. 85
Lent by Mr. and Mrs. Michael Blankfort

Schiele's paintings are essentially those of a great draftsman,
marked by the "thick" contours learned from his predeces-
sor Ferdinand Hodler. In his drawings this preference for the
powerful line led him to favor as media black chalk and
black crayon.

In *Two Standing Nudes* Schiele's assurance of line and his
psychological intensity are captured in the rhythmical
intertwining of the two bodies. The fulcrum point, as it
were, is the intersection of breast and arm in the center of
the group.

OSKAR SCHLEMMER
German, 1888–1943

66

Untitled (Profile), c. 1932 (ill. p. 101)
Watercolor
Signed by the artist's wife, on verso
21 x 15 in. (53.3 x 38.1 cm.)
Provenance: Dr. F. C. Valentien, Stuttgart; Schlesisches
Museum der bildenden Kunst, Breslau; Professor Ewald
W. Schnitzer, Los Angeles
Exhibitions: Frederick S. Wight Art Gallery, University of
California, Los Angeles, "German Expressionist Art, The
Robert Gore Rifkind Collection," February 27–April 17,
1977, No. 403
Literature: Orrel P. Reed, Jr., *German Expressionist Art, The
Robert Gore Rifkind Collection,* University of California, Los
Angeles, 1977, No. 403 (ill.)
Lent by The Robert Gore Rifkind Collection

For Oskar Schlemmer man with his perfect functions and
proportions was the "measure of all things." He conceived of
his role as an artist to be the search for a new ideal figure
which would reflect rational regularity and spiritual harmony
through man's gestures and movements. This essentially
classical ideal separated him from the German Expressionists
and from his colleagues at the Bauhaus: Klee, Feininger,
Kandinsky, Moholy-Nagy, and Albers.

Unlike the other Bauhaus artists, too, was Schlemmer's deep involvement with dance and the rhythms of human movement. Yet the movement in his art is hardly blatant. Rather, to use a musical analogy, it is a fugue, not a symphony, in which very few motifs are used to work out close harmonious relationships.

In *Profile* it is the vertical divisions which facet the head, arm, and background which create here, as in most of his works, a modulated rhythm, heightened by the tonal variations within the limited palette of blues and browns.

KURT SCHWITTERS
German, 1888–1948

67

Mz 390, 1930 (ill. p. 97)
Collage
Signed, bottom left: "Kurt Schwitters"; Titled and dated, bottom right: "Mz 390 1930"
Image: 7½ x 5½ in. (19 x 14 cm.); Paper: 8¾ x 6⅜ in. (22.2 x 16.2 cm.)
Provenance: Gertrude Stein Gallery, New York
Exhibitions: Annely Juda Gallery, London, "The Non-Objective World 1924–1939," July 7–September 30, 1971, No. 153A; Galleria Milano, Milan, 1971; Galerie Liatowitsch, Basel, "Die gegenstandslose Welt 1924–1939," February 5–March 15, 1972; La Jolla Museum of Contemporary Art, "Kurt Schwitters and Related Developments," March 9–May 6, 1973
Lent by Mr. and Mrs. M. A. Gribin

Hans Arp once said of his close friend Kurt Schwitters, "What nectar and ambrosia were to the Greek gods, glue was to Kurt Schwitters. Schwitters literally feasted on glue, and it was with glue that he produced his marvelous collages."[1] Poetic as the comment may be, it reveals Schwitters' preoccupation with collage, a form in which he was to be one of the foremost masters of the twentieth century. He was also a sculptor, typographer, and a talented writer; his collection of poems are prose pieces *Anna Blume* brought him international fame in 1919. But, it was in collage that Schwitters found that by using discarded objects he could create the abstractions which for him constituted art.

Both the Cubists and Futurists had used collage before Schwitters discovered it for himself in 1918–1919. He soon called his collages "Merz art" (after the last half of the word *Kommerz* which appeared in one of the early collages). In his collages, Schwitters turned his back on objective representation in favor of abstraction, accepting the use of any and all materials. What was done to these discarded objects in transfiguring them into art he called being Merzed.

Schwitters was closely associated with the Dada movement in the early 1920s and soon thereafter with the Constructivists whose interest in geometric forms is clearly evident in this rectilinear collage of 1930.

Schwitters labeled his small collages "Merz-zeichnungen" (Merz-drawings), which he abbreviated to Mz. Initially he numbered and dated them, but after 1926 he gave up the consecutive numbering, and after 1931 the numbers disappear entirely. In 1930, the year of this collage, there is a complete sequence of collages which seem to have been numbered all at once.[2]

[1] Quoted in Werner Schmalenbach, *Kurt Schwitters,* New York, 1967, p. 90.
[2] *Ibid*, p. 119.

GINO SEVERINI
Italian, 1883–1966

68

Still Life with Pipe, 1917 (ill. p. 80)
Pencil and watercolor
11¾ x 16½ in. (29.8 x 41.9 cm.)
Provenance: Burt Kleiner
Lent by the Los Angeles County Museum of Art, Gift of Burt Kleiner

Although Severini is known as a Futurist painter along with Balla and Boccioni, in 1917, the date of this watercolor, he was working in a Cubist vein. He continued to explore the simplified shapes and brighter colors of Synthetic Cubism until the early 1920s. In *Still Life with Pipe* he composes a still life of pipe, glass, and cards against a red and white striped oval background.

CHARLES SHEELER
American, 1883–1965

69

Bucks County Barn, 1926 (ill. p. 94)
Watercolor and pencil
6⅝ x 9⅛ in. (16.8 x 23.2 cm.)
Provenance: Downtown Gallery, New York
Exhibitions: Museum of Modern Art, New York, "Charles Sheeler," 1939, No. 73; University of California, Santa Cruz, "American Art of the 20's and 30's," April 17–May 12, 1973, No. 43
Literature: Museum of Modern Art, New York, *Charles Sheeler,* 1939, No. 73; *The Art Quarterly,* XXXV (Winter 1972), p. 442
Lent by the Fine Arts Gallery of San Diego, Bequest of Mr. Earle W. Grant

18 Charles Sheeler, *Bucks County Barn,* 1932, Museum of Modern Art, New York, Gift of Abby Aldrich Rockefeller

19 Charles Sheeler, *Architectural Cadences,* 1954, Whitney Museum of American Art, New York

Sheeler lived in his native Philadelphia until 1919. He studied at the Academy under William Merritt Chase and accompanied the older artist to Europe twice. After his return, he and a friend, Morton Schramberg, shared a small 1786 farmhouse in Doylestown in Bucks County on weekends. It was at this time that the interior of this house and the archetypal buildings of the countryside—barns, silos, farmhouses—were established as his basic subjects not only in paintings and drawings but in his photography as well.

One of the most famous of his early photographs is *Bucks County Barn* of 1915,[1] characteristic for its attention to the contrasts between highly lit sides and deep shadows; the textures of wood and rocks; and also to the shadows cast by unseen trees. Similar concerns are apparent in this small watercolor of 1926, marked by its freshness of observation. Six years later, in 1932, he used this watercolor as the basis for the large painting now in the Museum of Modern Art (fig. 18).

[1]Reproduced in Martin Friedman, *Charles Sheeler,* New York, 1975, p. 26.

70

Architectural Cadences, 1954 (ill. p. 94)
Watercolor and tempera
Signed, dated, and inscribed, bottom right: "To Joan and Fred Wight with deep appreciation Charles Sheeler 1954"
6¾ x 9⅛ in. (17.1 x 23.2 cm.)
Lent by Mr. and Mrs. Frederick S. Wight

Sheeler first evinced interest in the urban landscape after his move to New York City in 1919. By the 1940s industrial forms were dominant in his work, and by the mid-1940s he used multiple images in his research photographs, in his slides, and in his paintings. These industrial paintings combine the abstraction of Cubism and the literalness of the American tradition. In his paintings there are a number of paradoxes: value versus the two-dimensionality of form; descriptiveness versus generalization.

Architectural Cadences, like most of his works of the 1950s, is concerned with the prismatic effect of semi-transparent planes, a phenomenon he recorded in his slides as well. The watercolor was done after the painting (fig. 19) as a sketch for the serigraph produced in that same year. A comparison of the painting and watercolor reveals that Sheeler simplified the forms to make them read better on a small scale.

EVERETT SHINN
American, 1876–1953

71

Sixth Avenue Shoppers, c. 1910 (ill. p. 69)
Pastel and watercolor
Signed, bottom right: "E. Shinn"
20⅛ x 25¾ in. (51.1 x 65.4 cm.)
Provenance: James Graham Galleries, New York; Gift of Mrs. Sterling Morton to the Preston Morton Collection
Exhibitions: Oklahoma Art Center; Art Institute of Chicago, "Eleventh Annual Exhibition of Watercolors," 1932; Department of Fine Arts, University of Pittsburgh, 1959; New Jersey State Museum, "Everett Shinn, 1876–1953," circulated to Delaware Art Museum, Munson-

Williams-Proctor Institute, Oklahoma Art Institute, 1973–1974
Literature: Oklahoma Art Center, *Everett Shinn 1876–1953*, No. 69, p. 9; New Jersey State Museum, *Everett Shinn 1876–1953*, 1973, No. 70 (ill. p. 53)
Lent by the Santa Barbara Museum of Art, Preston Morton Collection

Everett Shinn, along with other members of The Eight—John Sloan, George Luks, and William Glackens—trained at the Pennsylvania Academy of Fine Arts under Thomas Anshutz and worked for many years as a newspaper reporter-artist. In 1897 he was the first of the four to move to New York City to work for the *New York World*. It was during the next year that he made his first pastel drawing since his student days. The story is recounted by Bernard Perlman in *The Immortal Eight*. After months of trying to have a drawing accepted for the center spread in *Harper's Weekly*, Shinn finally left a portfolio. Upon his return the editor, Colonel Harvey, asked to see him.

> "You have here such a variety of New York street scenes," the editor began, "that I was wondering if you have in your collection a large color drawing of the Metropolitan Opera House and Broadway in a snowstorm." Shinn glanced out of the window at the falling snow which would soon create the desired effect. "I think I have," he replied. "Good," snapped Harvey, "have it here at ten tomorrow morning."

> Shinn had his evening's work cut out for him. On his way home he purchased a fifty-cent box of pastels, then hurried to the Metropolitan Opera House to observe the architectural detail of its façade. Once home, he began to toy with the pastels…a medium he had not employed since his student days at the Pennsylvania Academy.

> Shinn worked through the early hours of the morning. Shaky and pale he delivered the finished drawing at the appointed deadline. Colonel Harvey stared at the artwork in silence. He scrutinized the lights twinkling dimly through the swirling snow, the dashing hansom cabs, the scurrying ladies hoisting their voluminous skirts. "We have to decide on a price," Harvey finally announced. "How about four hundred dollars and you own the original?"[1]

The story is illuminating; it reveals Shinn's facility as a rapid draftsman, his acute memory for details, and his approach to commissions.

Shinn's greatest achievement as a draftsman was his skill in handling the medium of pastel. Most of his best work during the early years of this century are drawings executed in pastel and watercolor. These were the works responsible for the fame which resulted from his first New York exhibition in 1900. Shinn developed a new technique in pastels. Edith DeShazo describes it well:

He took paper mounted on a heavy backing board and soaked it completely in a tub of water, removing excess water with his hand or a sponge. Then, with the final color composition completely in his mind, he began laying on patches of color. When these colors struck the wet ground, they turned immediately to a dark tone, losing their original coloration. Shinn worked swiftly and continued to build up his design until he had covered the whole surface. As the picture dried, the original color would return, but unlike the usual quality of pastel with its delicate, dustlike surface, evaporation of water caused the pigment to dry hard, producing brilliant color with a tempera-like quality."[2]

[1] Bernard Perlman, *The Immortal Eight*, New York, 1962, pp. 104–105.
[2] *Everett Shinn, 1876–1953*, New York, 1974, p. 157.

PAUL SIGNAC
French, 1863–1935

72

The Seine, Paris, 1910 (ill. p. 67)
Pencil and watercolor
Numbered, signed, and dated, bottom left: "13 Paul Signac, Sept. 1910"
10⅜ x 16½ in. (26.3 x 41.9 cm.)
Provenance: Purchased from the artist
Exhibitions: Los Angeles County Museum of Art, "Watercolors by Paul Signac," December 1953–January 1954, No. 2; Volkswagenwerk, Wolfsburg, Germany, "Französische Malerei von Delacroix bis Picasso," April–May 1961, No. 191
Literature: Los Angeles County Museum of Art, *Watercolors by Paul Signac*, 1953, No. 2 (ill.); Volkswagenwerk, Wolfsburg, Germany, *Französische Malerei von Delacroix bis Picasso*, 1961, No. 191, Pl. 99 (ill.)
Anonymous loan

Unlike the academicians of the early years of this century, Signac firmly believed in a watercolor technique in which most colors are separated from each other by the white of the paper; only through this technique could the true colors be captured. Moreover, he wrote, with watercolors, "it is not a question of establishing the scale of values, as with oil, but of suggesting them by equivalencies."[1]

Signac wrote in his book *Jongkind* of the relationship between watercolors and oil paintings: "Painting in oil is a severe struggle; watercolor is only a playful one."[2] For him watercolor was a means of quick notation which permitted a painter to expand his repertory through observations of such phenomena as cloud formations or the effects of a certain light. These notations later could be distilled into carefully planned and laboriously executed paintings. His watercolors have a spontaneity and liveliness totally lacking in his paintings, and very few of them were direct preparatory studies for the larger works. In them, however—as he noted of Jongkind's watercolors "with lively touches, he recreated the universe."[3]

[1]Paul Signac, *Jongkind*, Paris, 1927, p. 117.
[2]*Ibid.*, p. 117.
[3]*Ibid.*, p. 117.

DAVID SMITH
American, 1906–1965

73

Untitled, 1958 (ill. p. 129)
Brush and ink
Signed and dated, bottom right: "David Smith A 4/58 17"
16¾ x 21½ in. (42.5 x 54.6 cm.)
Provenance: G. David Thompson; B. C. Holland Gallery, Chicago
Exhibitions: Art Galleries, University of California, Santa Barbara, "7+5 Sculpture in the 1950's," January 6–February 15, 1976, circulated to Phoenix Art Museum, 1976
Literature: Phyllis Plous, *7+5 Sculpture in the 1950's,* University of California, Santa Barbara, 1976, No. 63 (ill.)
Lent by Mrs. Melville J. Kolliner

Like Maillol and Lachaise, David Smith was a prolific sculptor-draftsman. He explained why drawing was such an important activity for him:

> I make 300 to 400 large drawings a year, usually with egg yolk and Chinese ink and brushes. These drawings are studies for sculpture, sometimes what sculpture is, sometimes what sculpture can never be. Sometimes they are atmospheres from which sculptural form is unconsciously selected during the labor process of producing form. Then again they may be amorphous floating direct statements in which I am the subject, and the drawing is the act. They are all statements of my identity and come from the constant work stream. I title these drawings with the numerical noting of month, day, and year. I never intend a day to pass without asserting my identity: my work records my existence.[1]

This drawing of April 17, 1958, although not a direct preparatory drawing for a sculpture, is linked to Smith's sculpture of the same year in its exploration of movement and a swinging rhythm.

[1]*David Smith by David Smith: Sculpture and Writings,* London, 1968, p. 104.

JOSEPH STELLA
Italian/American, 1877–1946

74

Coal-Storage Tanks, c. 1920 (ill. p. 95)
Charcoal

Signed in charcoal, top right: "Joseph Stella"
21⅞ x 28 in. (55.5 x 71.1 cm.)
Provenance: Wright S. Ludington
Exhibitions: University of California, Santa Cruz, "American Art of the 20s and 30s," 1973
Literature: Irma Jaffe, *Joseph Stella,* Cambridge (Mass.), 1970 (Pl. 61)
Lent by the Santa Barbara Museum of Art, Gift of Wright S. Ludington (44.2.10)

Joseph Stella came to the United States in 1896 from Italy. Among his early work were very strong charcoal drawings of miners in Pittsburgh. From 1909 to 1913 he was in Europe and he returned highly enthusiastic about the advances of the Cubists and Futurists. In some of his paintings of the late teens, such as the famous *Brooklyn Bridge* of c. 1917–1918 (fig. 20), he uses the lines of force and the fusing of planes from Futurism. During these same years, his drawings show not a trace of this new style, and it is to the early Pittsburgh drawings that *Coal-Storage Tanks* relates.

The full title of the drawing is *The By-Products Storage Tanks that Receive the Distilled Ammonia and Tar from the Ovens.* It was made as an illustration for the article "The Coal By-Products Oven" which was published in *The Survey* on March 1, 1924. The drawing, according to Irma Jaffe, was made several years earlier, around 1921.[1] The motif was used again in the painting *Factories* now in the Art Institute of Chicago (fig. 21).

The strong, powerful drawing gives no indication of the horror Stella often felt about factories, whose power and energy later fascinated an artist like Sheeler. In *Brooklyn Bridge, A Page in My Life,* Stella wrote of a huge factory opposite his Brooklyn studio:

> ... its black walls scarred with red stigmas of mysterious battles.... was towering with the gloom of a prison. At night fires gave to innumerable windows menacing blazing looks of demons... Smoke, perpetually arising, perpetually reminded of war. One moved, breathed in an atmosphere of the impending Drama of Poe's tales. My artistic faculties were lashed to exasperation of production. I felt urged by a force to mould a compact plasticity, lucid as crystal that would reflect... the massive density, luridly accentuated by lightning, of the raging storm, in rivalry to Poe's granitic fiery transparency revealing the swirling horrors of the Maelstrom.[2]

[1]Irma Jaffe, *Joseph Stella*, Cambridge (Mass.), 1970, p. 60.
[2]*Ibid*, pp. 60–61.

75

Pink Flowers, c. 1919 (ill. p. 93)
Pencil and crayon
Signed, bottom right: "Joseph Stella"

11¾ x 7⅝ in. (29.8 x 19.3 cm.)
Provenance: Wright S. Ludington
Exhibitions: University of California, Santa Cruz, "American Art of the 20s and 30s," 1973
Literature: *American Watercolor Painting,* Watson Guptill, 1975
Lent by the Santa Barbara Museum of Art, Gift of Wright S. Ludington (45.8.31)

Drawings of flowers make up a large part of Stella's *oeuvre,* with literally hundreds of studies. His devotion to flowers is explained in his writings where he commented, "that all our days may glide by serene, sunny, each must begin with the study of a flower." Or, "my devout wish, that every working day might begin and end...as a good omen...with the light, gay painting of a flower."[1]

It is possible that Stella began making these studies in connection with the painting *Tree of Life* of 1919. There are many dated flower drawings from that year.

[1]Quoted in Irma Jaffe, *Joseph Stella,* Cambridge (Mass.), 1970, p. 85.

YVES TANGUY
French/American, 1900–1955

76

Untitled, 1943 (ill. p. 116)
Pencil and ink
Inscribed, signed and dated, bottom right: "pour Barbara, Yves Tanguy '43"
9⁷/₁₆ x 8½ in. (24 x 21.5 cm.)
Provenance: Gift of the artist
Lent by Mrs. Barbara R. Poe

In 1925, a year after the publication of the Surrealist Manifesto, Yves Tanguy met André Breton and became a member of the Surrealist group. He is noted, along with Dali and Magritte, for his Illusionistic Surrealism. In 1939 he came to America along with Matta and Ernst.

None of Tanguy's drawings are preparatory drawings for paintings. Only once did he attempt to follow the process of creating a painting after a drawing, for he said, "I found that if I planned beforehand, it never surprised me, and surprises are my pleasure in painting."[1] Moreover, such a process was alien to the Surrealists' belief in automatism.

As has been observed, Tanguy's drawings are "variations on the motif of recognizable shapes."[2] Similar real, if non-existent, objects inhabit Tanguy's dreamlike landscapes in which land melts into sky.

In this drawing of 1943 the detailed quality of the many finely-drawn lines around the edges of the objects prefigures

20 Joseph Stella, *Brooklyn Bridge,* 1917–1918, Yale University Art Gallery, Collection of Société Anonyme

21 Joseph Stella, *Factories,* Art Institute of Chicago, Gift of Mr. and Mrs. Noah Goldowsky in memory of Esther Goldowsky

22 Pavel Tchelitchew, *Hide-and-Seek* (detail), 1940–1942, Museum of
Modern Art, New York, Mrs. Simon Guggenheim Fund

the drawings of the late 1940s and 1950s with their myriad
small shapes clustered at the edges of the larger shapes.[3]

[1]Quoted in James Thrall Soby, *Yves Tanguy,* Museum of
Modern Art, New York, 1955, p. 17.
[2]Introduction by Nicolas Calas to *Yves Tanguy, Exhibition of
Gouaches and Drawings,* Pierre Matisse Gallery, New York,
1963, not paginated.
[3]Two other drawings of 1943 show this feathery treatment
of the edges. They are numbers 56 and 57 in the Matisse
Gallery exhibition. The catalogue also illustrates more than
ten late drawings of Tanguy.

PAVEL TCHELITCHEW
Russian/American, 1898–1957

77

Anatomical Head, 1945 (ill. p. 118)
Pen and ink
Signed and dated, bottom right: "P. Tchelitchew 45"
14 x 11⅛ in. (35.6 x 28.3 cm.)
Provenance: Catherine Viviano Gallery, New York
Lent by Mr. Jack Willis

Tchelitchew began his career in Russia as a Constructivist.
From 1923 when he arrived in Paris, he began to concentrate on the human head, face, and body. In 1929 he
made his first exploratory works which dealt with the interior of heads when he made four wax heads using ovoid
armatures. In each only the front was modeled while the
interior supports were left visible as negative images of
the features. It was in his large painting *Hide-and-Seek* of
1941–1942 (fig. 22) that he began to explore the interiors
of bodies. In 1941 he also designed costumes for the ballet
(never produced) *The Cave of the Sleep.* His costumes would
have included elements from the muscular, nervous, lym-
phatic, and arterial systems.

In the drawings of 1942–1947, which he called "interior
landscapes," Tchelitchew explored the anatomical interiors
of heads and bodies. Lincoln Kirstein has called them
"portraits of places": "Sometimes the place is the antrim,
the vault of the sinus, the spiral labyrinth of inner ear,
corridors of the semicircular canal, the tree of the nervous
system, rivers of lymph and blood, or pools of glands
and vessels."[1]

[1]Lincoln Kirstein, *Pavel Tchelitchew,* Gallery of Modern Art,
New York, 1964, p. 43.

LEON TUTUNDJIAN
Hungarian, 1905–1968

78

Untitled, c. 1924 (ill. p. 96)
Pencil
Initialed, bottom right: "LHT"
10⅛ x 8 in. (25.7 x 20.4 cm.)
Provenance: Ansley Graham Gallery, Los Angeles
Lent by Mr. and Mrs. M. A. Gribin

Leon Tutundjian left his native Hungary for Paris in the
1920s. In the early 1930s he became a Surrealist and
remained faithful to that style until his death.

His drawings of the 1920s are notable for their delicacy.
Here the mist of graphite surrounding the "bullet-hole" is
reminiscent of Kandinsky's use of watercolor sprays in his
work. The drawing achieves its pictorial effect through the
combination of mist and thin lines.

MAURICE de VLAMINCK
French, 1876–1958

79

Landscape, c. 1925 (ill. p. 84)
Pen and ink, and watercolor
Signed, bottom right: "Vlaminck"
17½ x 21¼ in. (44.5 x 54 cm.)
Provenance: Purchased from the artist in 1925
Anonymous loan

Vlaminck won his first and most lasting fame as a Fauvist
painter. By 1911 his palette had become darker, and his style
looser, marked by sweeping brushstrokes.

Of nature, Vlaminck once commented revealingly: "One
does not flirt with Nature; one possesses her. One must pen-
etrate her very being."[1] His landscapes are permeated
by a sober passion; seemingly nondescript scenes of roads
and houses are activiated by a sense of movement and
throbbing life.

[1]Jean Selz, *Vlaminck,* New York, 1966, p. 79.

Paul Signac
The Seine, Paris
1910

George Bellows
Street Scene
c. 1910

Everett Shinn
Sixth Avenue Shoppers
c. 1910

35

34

Käthe Kollwitz
Studies of Men
1908

Käthe Kollwitz
Bust-length Portrait of a Woman with Folded Arms
1904

58

28

Max Pechstein
Resting Woman with Mirror
1910

Ernst Ludwig Kirchner
Man and Woman
c. 1908

Erich Heckel
Kneeling Nude Woman
1913

Frantíšek Kupka
Flower
c. 1925

Franz Marc
Colored Flowers
1914

Egon Schiele
The Embrace
1915

41

August Macke
Women at the Zoo
1914

Egon Schiele
Two Standing Nudes
1918

Gustav Klimt
Two Standing Female Nudes
c. 1918

Lyonel Feininger
Vollersroda
1918

František Kupka
Dynamisme
1912

Gino Severini
Still Life with Pipe
1917

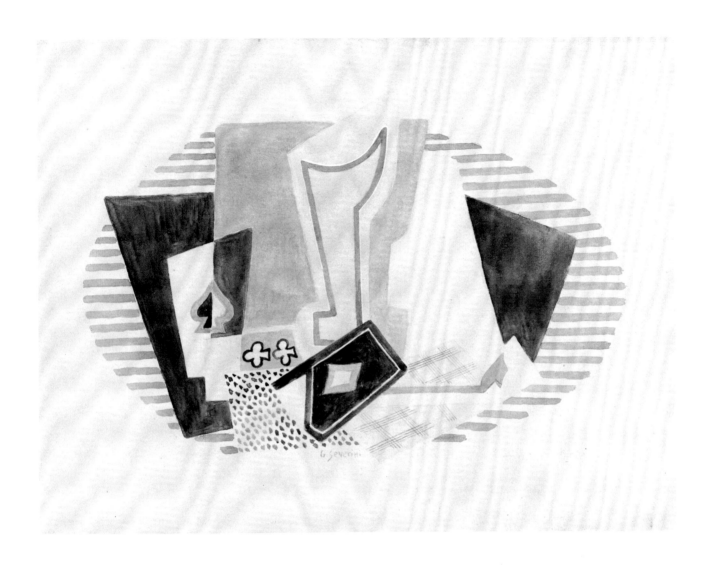

6

Giorgio de Chirico
Metaphysical Interior with Fish Molds
1916

19

Albert Gleizes
Composition with Two Nudes
1920

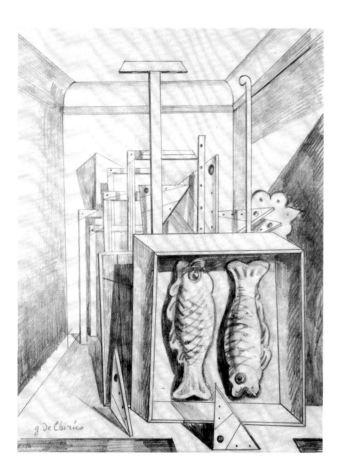

Amadeo Modigliani
Portrait of François Bernouard
1917–1918

Wyndham Lewis
Portrait of Olivia Shakespear
1920

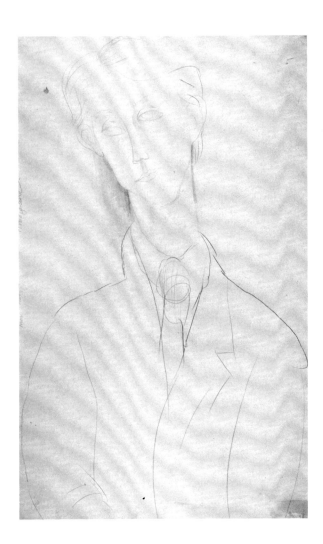

Marc Chagall
Card Players
1917

Maurice de Vlaminck
Landscape
c. 1925

Pablo Picasso
Italian Peasants
1919

Jacob Epstein
Head of a Negress
c. 1925

Henri Matisse
Reclining Nude
c. 1922–1923

Gaston Lachaise
Standing Nude with Drape
c. 1927

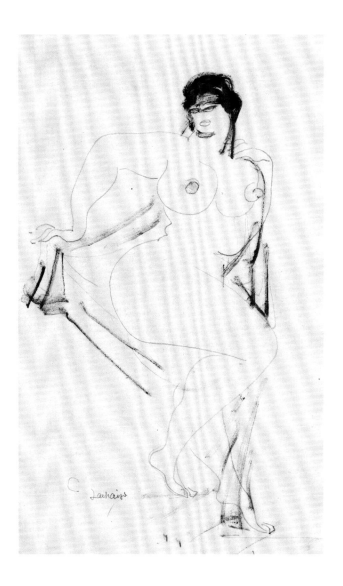

27

Augustus John
Seated Nude
c. 1923

42

Aristide Maillol
Reclining Female Nude
c. 1920

Maurice Prendergast
Picnic
c. 1915

Charles Demuth
Sailboats (The Love Letter)
1919

Elie Nadelman
Three Birds
c. 1920

11

75

Charles Demuth
Lilacs in a Vase
c. 1925

Joseph Stella
Pink Flowers
c. 1919

69
Charles Sheeler
Bucks County Barn
1926

70
Charles Sheeler
Architectural Cadences
1954

74
Joseph Stella
Coal-Storage Tanks
c. 1920

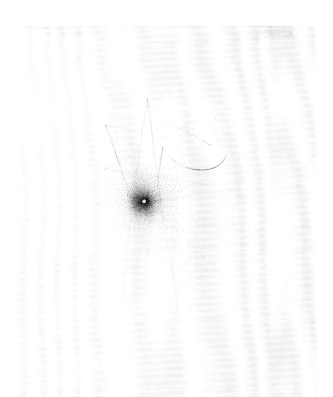

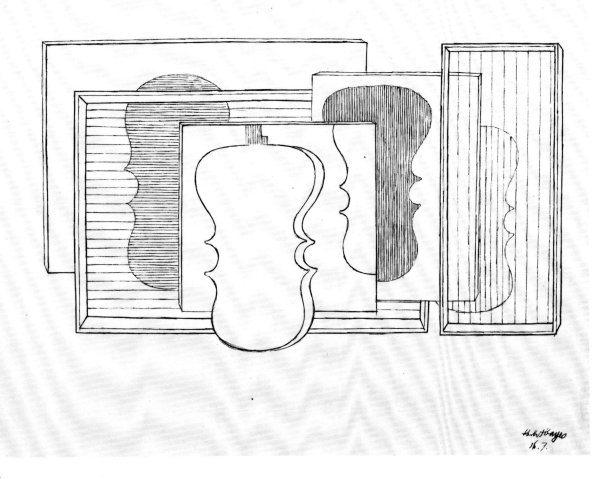

Kurt Schwitters
Mz 390
1930

Paul Klee
Bunt Fenestes an der Lage gemessen
(Stained-Glass Windows in a Precise Position)
1928

Paul Klee
Scheren-gitter und seine Feindin
(Rail Fence and His Enemy)
1940

Max Ernst
Two Doves
1927

Oskar Schlemmer
Untitled (Profile)
c. 1932

Emil Nolde
North German Landscape

Emil Nolde
Red and Gold Sunflowers

Emil Nolde
Lovers (Portrait of the Artist and His Wife)
1932

George Grosz
Broadway
1934

Georges Rouault
Ballerina and Two Clowns
c. 1930

Pablo Picasso
Woman Before a Mirror
1934

Henri Matisse
Head of a Woman, Number 1
1937

Henri Matisse
Still Life with Fruit
1941

Joan Miro
La femme au collier
(Woman with Necklace)
1937

Salvador Dali
Grotesque Heads
c. 1936

John Steuart Curry
Storm over Lake Otsego
c. 1925

Thomas Hart Benton
Saturday Afternoon
c. 1939

13
14
21

Arthur Dove
Out the Window
c. 1940

Arthur Dove
Centerport Series, #2
c. 1941

Arshile Gorky
Study for Nighttime, Enigma and Nostalgia
1931–1932

Julio Gonzales
Study for a Sculpture
1941

Yves Tanguy
Untitled
1943

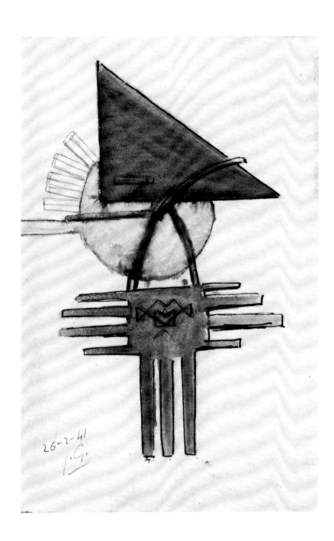

Matta (Roberto Matta Echaurren)
Untitled
c. 1940

Pavel Tchelitchew
Anatomical Head
1945

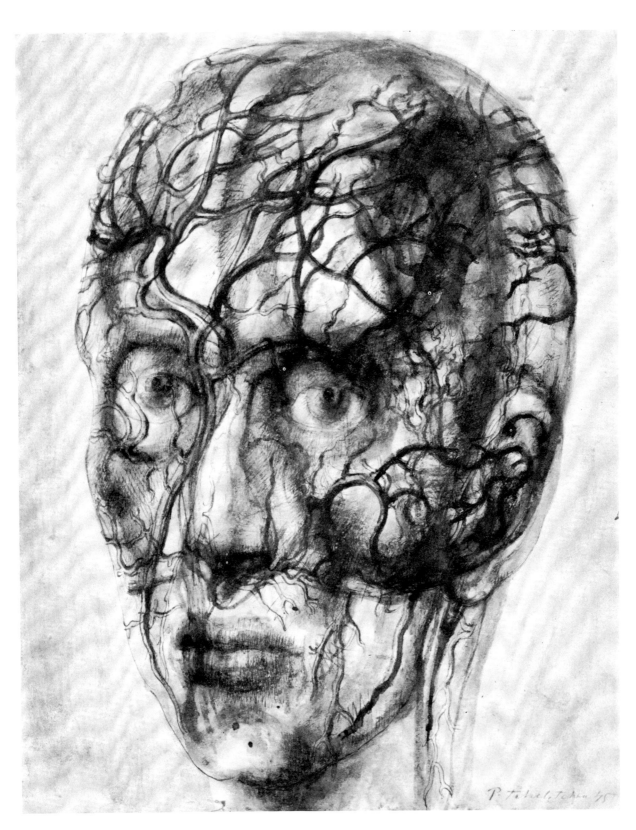

Rico Lebrun
Sunflower
1947

Milton Avery
Seaside Haircut
1948

Robert Motherwell
Displaced Table
1943

Arshile Gorky
Study for Liver is the Cock's Comb
1943

Jackson Pollock
Number 4
1948

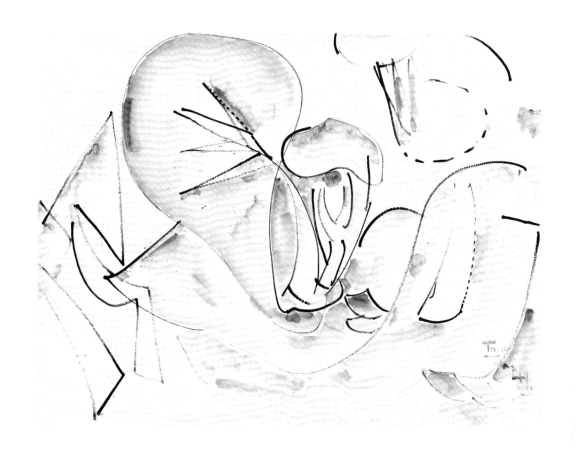

125

Robert Motherwell
Spanish Elegy (Molina de Segura)
1953

Franz Kline
Untitled
1953

9
Willem de Kooning
Woman
1952

24
Philip Guston
Untitled
1954

128

David Smith
Untitled
1958

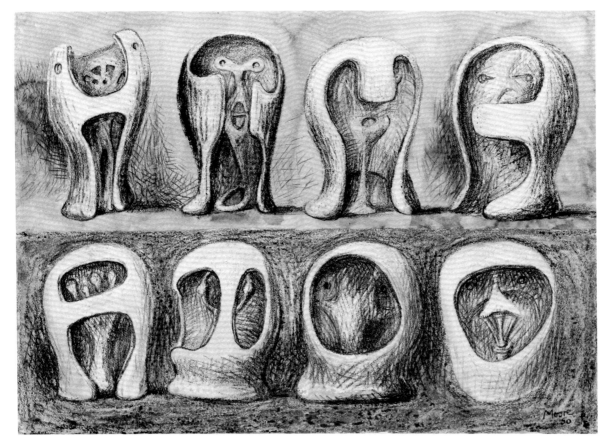

Giorgio Morandi
Still Life of Bottles
1957

Henry Moore
Heads (No. 2) (Interior and Exterior Forms)
1950

Richard Diebenkorn
Seated Nude
1960

132